Stepping into Rural Wisconsin

Stepping into Rural Wisconsin

GRANDPA CHARLY'S LIFE VIGNETTES, FROM PRUSSIA TO THE MIDWEST

Edward J. Kuehn and Linda T. Ruggeri

The Insightful Editor
565 Pier Ave
Suite 1008
Hermosa Beach, CA 90254-9998
www.theinsightfuleditor.com
www.facebook.com/ruralwisconsinthebook

Library of Congress Control Number: 2017912139
Published by Linda Ruggeri

ISBN-13: 9780999278000
ISBN-10: 0999278002

This book is dedicated to my brother Carl, who passed away before it was finished.
Edward J. Kuehn

To my father, for teaching me to be a voracious reader.
Linda T. Ruggeri

Contents

Introduction

I OFTEN VISITED MY SISTER Alice on Saturday mornings. She would always have a folder of saved articles along with a list of topics to remind her of what she wanted to talk about with me. This particular day, the items were on the dining room table, and she handed them to me as I was leaving, ready to go home. My other sister, Elaine, had already looked through them. Now it was my turn to review them and dispose of them as I saw fit. At a first glance, I could tell these weren't just old papers, but documents with a historical and familial significance. These two thick envelopes once belonged to our paternal grandfather.

I was 74 when this journey of discovering my paternal grandfather's life began.

Of the envelopes, one contained an abstract for real estate transactions in Ripon, dating back to 1854, when the city was being plotted. The documents described land parcels, financial transactions and mentioned the names of individuals and families involved, providing me with an intersecting point of two storylines. From a technical perspective, a documented history of land deals for a portion of the City of Ripon, including land our grandfather would later come to own. And, from an emotional perspective, a storyline for our family's history in Wisconsin, their whereabouts and doings. This farmstead abstract explained how things unfolded that I had never really thought about when I was younger and living in Ripon. But more importantly, it told me the story of someone I looked up to, loved and quietly admired, my grandfather Charly.

This farm is where I got to know my grandparents. By looking at these deeds and abstracts, interlacing them with my memories of my relatives, searching through long stored away family photos (and really looking at the photos this time), they all sparked questions and created conversations with my siblings and cousins that I had never had before. My grandparent's farm purchase in Ripon, impacted the whole immediate family and the generations that came after. Thanks to that farm, and the people who lived there, I'm here today writing these stories.

After extensive genealogy research, many eager days and long nights thinking about who my grandparents really were, I wanted to recreate, through drawings and photos, what their farmstead might have looked like and how it evolved as improvements were made to accommodate an ever-growing family. This led to writing down notes, with personal memories and anecdotes I had, to help me construct a more complete picture of them. Again, this book is based on my memories and conversations with family members. When there were gaps of information, I've filled them with what I believe happened based solely on my research of rural Wisconsin life at the time (and it is noted so in the text).

The first result of my research produced a short book intended solely for my family, mainly transcribing the handwritten mortgage abstract[1], with a few personal sketches and black and white period photos of my grandparents. It was a very technical piece, but it served as the backbone for the broader vignette-like story I wanted to tell based on my recollections. My grandparents were good, hardworking people, like those that made up the thread of America. Their story could be considered by today's standards uneventful, undecorated but one of honest success. When placed in the context of local,

---

1 The transcribed abstract is available online at www.theinsighfuleditor.com/portfolio

national or world history, their story became to me more profound, more interesting and had greater value.

The story of my grandparents is like that of so many other American's, one of immigration, struggles, language barriers, never ending hard work, incalculable sacrifice, and a large family that needed to be nourished, educated, and launched into the world as good citizens carrying the family name. My grandparent's history is my history. Their blood is my blood. And at the end of the day, their story has become my story too.

Edward J. Kuehn

CHAPTER 1

Coming Back Home on the Texas Chief

‿ᧁ

Composite illustration of the Texas Chief approaching the Temple,
Texas train station in the 1950s. Rendering by author.

TUESDAY, JUNE 6, 1956. AFTER traveling for forty-five minutes in a bus without air conditioning, it felt good to finally get off, stretch my legs, and find a restroom when we got to the Temple, Texas train station.

The weather was quite hot for that early in summer, and the mixed smell of diesel, burnt rubber and smog-covered asphalt seemed to emanate like steam from the parking lot. My clothes had already wrinkled and I was sweating, even though the day had just begun. This was my first summer in Texas and I was oblivious to the hot weather and humidity that was yet to come.

Earlier that morning, I had been called into the First Sergeant's office. I was still feeling edgy after our unexpected meeting. In the past couple of weeks my mother had sent letters to him directly, asking that I be allowed to come home for my brother's graduation. Graduating from high school was a big event in our family, and especially this one, since my youngest brother Carl would be the last child of my parents to finish high school. Two months earlier, in April, I had missed my sister Elaine's wedding because my three-day pass had been denied. Per the Army, at that time, I was *in transit*, moving from where I had been originally stationed in Maryland to Texas, the same weekend the wedding was to take place.

First Sergeant Moses had already called me into his office a couple of times before regarding my mother's letters. He insisted I needed to make sure she understood, as he said, "*this isn't some sort of summer camp I'm running here! You're in the Army now, soldier!*"

As I entered the orderly room that morning the company clerk, using a matter of fact tone, said "*Go right in. Sergeant Moses is expecting you.*" I could tell nothing good was going to come of this. Having been chewed out during those earlier office visits, I was anticipating another unpleasant experience having to justify my mother's unrelenting behavior. It didn't help that I also felt intimidated by the rank on his sleeve: three chevrons up, three rockers down with a diamond in the middle, the insignia of a first sergeant.

I, on the other hand, had nothing on my sleeves.

What have I done wrong now? I kept wondering. His stare met my eyes and he said, "at ease." Then, in a fatherly tone of voice, he told me I had been given a leave because my family requested I come home. My grandfather, Charles Kuehn, had passed away and The American Red Cross had arranged for a permission of a ten-day emergency leave so I could attend his funeral, adding "You better hurry; if not you'll miss your travel connections, and you won't get there in time."

Leaving the first sergeant's office I rushed to the barracks and packed my AWOL bag with some civilian clothes, a toothbrush, shaving gear, a hairbrush, and a change of underwear.

It seemed to take a long time for the Army's post bus, with all the stops, to get to the station in Killeen. The layover should have been short, but it dragged on forever as I waited for a civilian bus to take me to the train station in Temple. I had begun the trip in Fort Hood as early as possible and now it was already getting to be late in the forenoon.

The ride to the Temple Train Station went smoothly and upon arriving I anxiously looked around for the ticket window, never having had purchased a ticket here before. The train I needed to catch stopped only once a day and would be arriving soon. If I missed it, I'd have to wait another whole day. To get a military discount on the train ticket, I had put on my Army-issued summer uniform: khaki pants and shirt, made of chino material. The pants were plain, without pleats or cuffs, the shirt long sleeved (even in summer), with button down flaps over the two breast pockets and epaulets at the shoulders. An olive drab colored web belt with a brass buckle held the pants. A tie was not required uniform attire when traveling. I had only been in the Army for a few months so my uniform was "slick sleeved."[2] The exception being the unit patch sewn on the left sleeve at the shoulder, which represented the Fourth Army. It had a white four-leafed clover, stem pointing down, on a red background. On each collar point of the shirt, a round brass badge was pinned with the initials "US" on the right, and on the left side the branch insignia. I was in the Ordnance corp.[3] Our insignia was a cannonball with a flame shooting out of the top. Old-timer soldiers said it looked like a spittoon that was on fire, while others crudely called it the "flaming piss pot."

The only other color on the uniform was a crimson braid, the Ordnance Corps color, sewn on the edges of the khaki garrison cap. The brown oxford shoes with brown socks I had been issued, completed my mandatory uniform.

---

2 The term "Slick Sleeved" referred to the uniform of a service member who had not been in service long enough to have earned any stripes that would be sewn onto the sleeves.

3 The U.S. Army Ordnance Corps and School is a Sustainment branch of the U.S. Army, headquartered at Fort Lee, Virginia. Their duty is to supply Army combat units with weapons and ammunition, including at times their procurement and maintenance. Source: http://www.goordnance.army.mil

My brother Carl (left, age 19) and me (right, age 21), on active duty in the Army. I was stationed at Fort Hood, Texas while Carl was stationed at Fort Carson, Colorado. The Fourth Army patch is shown on the left shoulder of my uniform and the Ordnance insignia on my left collar. Kuehn Family Collection.

The train station seemed a busy world on its own. I was conscious that I was representing the Army, and this kept me vigilant. I noticed that although there were two waiting areas, most of the people were seated in the larger one. The sign at the entrance to the smaller room was my first experience with segregation. "Colored" it read. I had grown up in a small rural community in Wisconsin and was obviously a bit naive. Even though I had heard about segregation, now I was seeing it in real time. Adding to my confusion was that in the Army, differences in skin color didn't matter. We worked together, lived together, took care of and looked out for each other. We were all equals.

Besides my first exposure to segregation, I was dealing with my own maturing identity. In the seven months I had been in the Ordnance Corps I could feel I had changed. There was no one in my immediate family or circle of friends who had served, so I had no one to talk to about life in the Army.

During the first few months I didn't have to make decisions because I was herded along with all the others. First, learning how to "soldier" in basic training and then, going to school to learn a job skill. In that short time I was being indoctrinated with Army values. I was making the transition to think militarily. I had never been away from home this long either, it was all new to me and I was going at it alone.

Four months had passed since my last visit home. During that time, I was assigned to Fort Hood, Texas, my permanent duty station. Something about being there made me feel proud. Texas has a special aura about it, and if one wishes to, you can indulge in the swagger. Remembering I wasn't too far removed from just being a farm boy however, kept me grounded.

The sound of music coming from the other end of the station brought me back to where I was. Those lyrics... they were vaguely familiar. After buying my ticket, I wandered over to see where the music was coming from. A jukebox in the back corner of the station's restaurant channeled nostalgia. It was a family-type restaurant offering the traditional American diner experience. Sandwiches, hamburgers, French fries, soft drinks and coffee - America's primary hot beverage. For dessert option a slice of pie or ice cream, similar to what one would find in a Woolworth's or Kresge's dime store lunch counter of that era. A slice of fresh homemade pie sure did sound good at that moment, but I couldn't treat myself to that luxury.

The song lyrics added to my uneasiness, "*Well... I... never felt more like singing the blues...*"[4] It was a new song I had only heard once or twice before, but I liked it. The lyrics told the story of a young man who had broken up with his girlfriend and was feeling blue. I too was feeling blue, but I hadn't broken up with my girlfriend. I didn't even have one. A girlfriend would have to come later. I couldn't afford one nor did I have time to go on dates. I was in the Army and my military obligations came first. Besides, I was pretty bashful.

The wooden bench I was sitting on felt hard and uncomfortable. How many others like me had sat there waiting for a train, unknowingly polishing it? That song continued to nag me. Someone must have kept pushing nickels into the Jukebox because it played over and over and over again. The opening chords and the first few words embedded themselves in my mind.

> *Well, I never felt more like singin' the blues*
> *'Cause I never thought that I'd ever lose*
> *Your love dear, why'd you do me this way*
> *Well, I never felt more like cryin' all night*
> *'Cause everything's wrong, there ain't nothin' right*
> *With-out you, you got me singin' the blues...*

I was listening to the music and thinking about going home when the noise of an approaching train jarred me back to reality. I dashed out to the platform, to the direction of the sound. There it was, the Texas Chief, rolling down the tracks towards me.

The train announced its presence, not with a high-pitched whistle but, with a masculine air horn, as if coming from deep within its gut. A sound like that of an animal warding off others from its fresh kill. The sound one would expect from a train engine with the word TEXAS in its

---

4 "Singing the Blues" was a popular song written by Melvin Endsley in 1956. The song was first recorded and released by Marty Robbins in 1956.

name. I was awestruck by the size of the imposing beast, the rumble of its diesel engines, the smell of the exhaust and screeching of the brakes as it slowed. It only had twelve to fifteen cars, those essential for passenger needs: sleepers, compartment cars, a restaurant, a mail car, and a baggage car or two. The Texas Chief was short but powerful.

When I approached to board, the agent looked at my ticket and directed me to a coach car. I walked past the nice cars, which were further away from the bustling noise of the engine, to find my place in the cheaper seats of coach. I entered my section and chose a window seat where I could be alone and watch the scenery. Not a lot of people were leaving for northern destinations on that Tuesday morning. I pushed my duffle bag under the seat in front of me so I could keep an eye on it.

The train didn't stay long at the Temple station. I had no more than gotten settled in when I felt the car jerk and the clanking of the slack when it was taken up in the connections between the cars. The train began to move and the on-board conductor came by checking tickets. He looked at mine to see where I would be getting off, then said "you'll be on the train throughout the night son, so make yourself as comfortable as possible." Because I was a Private in the Army I couldn't pay to travel in a sleeper car. It would be next morning by the time we arrived at the final stop, the end of the line in Chicago.

I should have been able to relax since I had made all my connections, but now an overwhelming feeling of melancholy set in. Alone with my thoughts, I had all the time in the world to answer my life's question marks. Stillness usually forces thinking, and my mind wandered back to what I had felt for the first time in the train station waiting room, an identity conflict of sorts. I hadn't been in the Army too long, but it was long enough to know I was becoming a different person.

Well... I...never felt more like singing the blues...
...without you, you got me singing the blues
...without you, you got me singin' the blues....

Outside the scenery was moving past faster and faster. The wide-open countryside, vast and empty, was dotted with a few lonely grazing cattle. As the train whistled through small shabby towns without stopping, I noticed each one had a grain elevator and occasionally a cattle feedlot, just like at home in Wisconsin. By early afternoon the train had arrived in Fort Worth, Texas for another stopover.

After leaving Fort Worth, the remainder of the day passed uneventfully. I walked from passenger car to passenger car to pass the time and break through the monotony. As daylight gave way to dusk I looked at my watch. According to the schedule, we should now be traveling through Oklahoma and would soon enter Kansas, the sunflower state.

When darkness came upon us, the coach lights were dimmed and I saw my reflection in the window. Seeing myself made me pause - how much had changed in these last few months. My feelings couldn't settle, the rocking motion of the train and the rhythmic click clack of wheels passing over rail joint bars should have lulled me to sleep, but they didn't. Thoughts bounced back and forth between the time I lived at home as a teenager, before I joined the Army, and now this person I was in the U.S. Ordnance Corps. Images of my grandfather, a man who had seen me grow up, and who now wouldn't be there to talk to. I couldn't share with him all the new things I was learning. Not that we had long, profound conversations often, but he cared about us in his own way. Alternating thoughts of being in Ripon and visiting his farm, were juxtaposed with the reality that I was now living with strangers who were quickly becoming my new family.

The questions kept coming up. One after the other. There were so many things I didn't know about myself, about my family. It took leaving them to start thinking about them. Who were they really, and who was I? Who had my grandfather been? It never occurred to me to ask about my grandparents' story. I had naively assumed they would always be there. I spent that long train ride processing so many contradicting feelings, but kept returning to the thought that I was coming back home to be with Grandpa Charly one last time, at his funeral.

CHAPTER 2

A Step Back

The Princeton Monthly Fair brought city and country
people together to buy and sell merchandise and cattle.
March 1908. Courtesy Princeton Historical Society.

1894 WAS A BUSY YEAR in the world. In Europe, Britain established a pro-
tectorate over Uganda, Manchester City Football Club was formed in
England, and London's Tower Bridge opened to vehicle traffic for the
first time. Sir William Ramsay and Lord Rayleigh discovered Argon, the
first noble gas. Russian emperor Alexander III was succeeded by his son

Nicholas II, who unknown at the time, would be the last tsar to rule Russia. In Asia, the Bubonic Plague hit Hong Kong claiming a death toll of 2,255 people; and New Zealand enacted the world's first minimum wage law.

In North America, the Great Hinckley Forest Fire in Minnesota claimed the lives of more than 450 people. 1894 was also the year of three big strikes in the U.S.: In New York City, 12,000 tailors struck against sweatshop working conditions; a coal miners' strike closed mines across the central United States for 8 weeks (with unsuccessful results); and in Illinois 3,000 factory workers from the Pullman Palace Car Company, which fabricated hotel cars, parlor cars, sleeper and diner railroad cars, went on a "wildcat" strike - without union approval. Oil is discovered on the Osage Indian reservation (present day Kansas), making the Osage the "richest group of people in the world" at that time. Poet E. E.Cummings, American film director John Ford and comedian Jack Benny are born, and Coca-Cola is sold for the first time in bottles.

Locally, the state of Wisconsin was taking part in The Progressive Era, which had just begun a year earlier in 1893: "...numerous products manufactured in Wisconsin, such as agricultural implements, fanning mills, leather goods, sashes and doors and beer, were on the verge of attaining national markets and reputations... Although its forests were being depleted at an alarming rate, Wisconsin was still the nation's foremost lumbering state."[5]

In terms of population supporting that growth, history books show that like other states in the US, Wisconsin had become a mix of natives and newcomers. The original Wisconsinites were Native Americans who had concentrated themselves into 4 tribes: the Chippewa, a mixed group of Chippewa and Ottawa and Potawatomi, the Menominee and, the Winnebago. However, by the mid-1800s they were being required to cede their land to the federal government, a time when Wisconsin was on its way to achieve its statehood (in 1848).

---

5 Buenker, John D. *The History of Wisconsin, Volume IV, The Progressive Era, 1893-1914,* Madison, Wis., Historical Society of Wisconsin, p.1-2.

Wisconsin had a strong population of Native Americans. During the fur trade era, 1500s-1700s, tribes such as the Fox, Kickapoo, Miami, Sauk and Mascoutin were present from northern Illinois, all through the north of Wisconsin, along with fur traders. But the first true migration wave occurred when Yankees came from the East Coast (New England, New York, Pennsylvania, and Ohio specifically.) "Endowed with capital and skills, well versed in pioneering and the workings of federal land laws, and experienced in government and politics, Yankees quickly seized control of Wisconsin's socio-economic engine"[6].

During that same period of Indian land cessions and Yankee arrival, a second wave of immigration was coming into Wisconsin, this time from northern and western Europe. These people were looking for the state and nation's economic promise, arriving from separate areas of the former Prussian kingdom such as Posen, West Prussia, Pomerania, and Brandenburg[7]. "By 1890, three-fourths of all Wisconsinites were either immigrants or the children of foreign-born parents."

In rural Wisconsin, these changes were observed on a smaller scale as opposed to the great movements taking place in urban and industrialized areas such as Milwaukee or Green Bay, the latter having one of the first Registers for the US Land Office where people came to buy unclaimed federal land from the government. This was the office used by Green Lake[8] and Fond du Lac County settlers.

We know through local history books that the Menominee and Winnebago Indians (these last ones later known as the Ho-Chunk) spent part of their time in the Green Lake County[9] area, where my own memories formed, but were being slowly pushed out, while settlers, mostly from the east coast, were beginning to buy and plat land locally.

---

6 Buenker, John D. *The History of Wisconsin, Volume IV, The Progressive Era, 1893-1914*, p.180.

7 Podoll, Brian, C.G.R.S., *Prussian Netzelanders and Other German Immigrants in Green Lake, Marquette & Waushara Counties, Wisconsin*. Heritage Books, Inc.

8 Heiple, Robert and Emma, *A Heritage History of Beautiful Green Lake*. Richard Dart makes a reference to this office in his recount *Settlement of Green Lake County*.

9 Green Lake County was part of Marquette County, until 1858 when it became its own county.

When the former generations of my family emigrated from Posen (Prussia) to Princeton, Wisconsin, all the above was simultaneously taking place in the world.

October 31 of that same year, 1894, would be the beginning of a new life for my grandfather, Carl August Kuehn. He was a first-generation Wisconsinite. The day after his 24th birthday he married sixteen-year-old Hulda Theresa Bandt in Princeton, Wisconsin. I know this not because of family storytelling; nobody spoke about my grandparent's marriage, ever. The few living relatives I still have knew only minor details about our family's past. I searched for archived records at the Green Lake and Fond du Lac County (Wisconsin) Register of Deeds, as well as any other lead or possible source of information. It was a journey in and of itself to unearth relevant material regarding my paternal grandparents, an attempt to find the missing pieces of my family's history puzzle.

Their only wedding photo to survive was discovered by my cousin Jeannie in her mother's, my aunt Meita's, memorabilia. I've spent an untold amount of time looking at that wedding photo, as if hoping my grandparents image would talk to me, revealing something new. I analyzed their facial expressions, then their clothing, and the surrounding background in the setting. They clearly weren't outdoors, after all it was late October in Wisconsin, too cold to be outside. It had to be a studio photograph. Photo equipment was too cumbersome to cart around back then. It had been staged with a country setting background. I tried hard to uncover any details that might reveal something about their late 1800s personas - including discussing the photo with local historical society staff members, curators of social history, including historical bridal gown experts.

Although some women married in white during the late 19th century (mostly those of wealthy families), many wore black or other

My grandparents wedding photo, October 31, 1894. Hulda wears a
dark (probably) velvet A-line gown, with leg of mutton sleeves. White
velvet accents on the collar, waistband, cuffs of sleeves and hemline.
A cathedral length veil adorned with a coronet of (most likely) small
orange blossom flowers completes her dress. Kuehn Family Collection.

colors so the dress could also be used for "visiting" or special occasions. Charles most likely used his only suit, the one reserved for
church or social festivities. The following day - November 1, 1894 -
The weekly Princeton Republic, carried a short article announcing
their marriage.

—Charles Kuehn and Miss Huldah Bants were married yesterday afternoon at the German Methodist church, Rev. Barowski officiating. The Republic extends congratulations to the happy couple.

My grandparents wedding announcement. Note the misspelling of Hulda's first and last name (misspelling was a common occurrence in this era). Courtesy Caestecker Public Library, Green Lake, Wisconsin.

I always wondered why my grandparents married on a Wednesday. When researching my family's history, I discovered how essential it was to place myself in the context of the times and think about behaviors, actions and decisions being made based on *practicality*. As I would soon learn, the day a wedding ceremony was conducted depended upon the availability of the clergy who at that time, in rural areas, may have been obliged to cover multiple churches with varying sacramental needs. What's more, my grandparents' marriage does not appear to have been a hurried affair, considering they were nicely dressed and had a studio photographer record their event.

"The time and place of a wedding were largely determined by convenience. November, December, and January were the most popular months in which to marry... Farm obligations were less pressing than during the summer. A couple issued verbal invitations to family and friends, who gathered in the morning at the minister's home or in the bride's parlor; few weddings occurred in churches... Whatever the location or time, however, the ceremony was the same... a ritualized affirmation of family. Everyone had an obligation to support and nurture the new family unit."[10]

---

10 From *Courtship and Marriage in the 18th Century*, www.history.org.

We don't know which family bore the costs of the wedding, the fees for the clergy, the use of the church and any other expenditures. Traditionally the bride's family would cover these expenses as their contribution to the newlyweds beginning a life of their own. There is no anecdotal record of whether Charles's or Hulda's family provided a dowry to help them get started, but it is possible, as I learned after reviewing detailed tax rolls, that Hulda's parents were the most likely able to provide financial support to them at that time.

None of my family stories talk about how my grandparents met or how long they knew each other before getting married. Their own parents, my great-grandparents, were European immigrants who settled in Princeton, Wisconsin in different years. Charles and Hulda were the first generation of their respective families to be born in the United States. Somehow they had come to know each other the small town of Princeton[11].

Looking back, and pondering this in the context of the times, a rural setting, the inconvenience of travel and lack of privacy at one's home, what was that first encounter like? More than likely, both families attended the same neighborhood German Methodist church where Charles and Hulda later married. The church was within an approximate five-mile radius from Fred Bandt's farm.

Young Charles may have worked as a hired farm hand for one of the other Kuehn families living in the area (there were 3 Kuehn families who owned land in Princeton township at the time, none of them being Charles' father.) Or, perhaps he worked for Hulda's father instead. Back then, hired help lived in the house with the employing family if they were single, with room and board typically considered part of their compensation. If that were the case, they would have come to know each other in a most convenient setting. Another possibility is that Hulda herself might have been employed to help with housework for a close neighbor of Charles' family or even his own family. Sharing help was a common practice when all hands

---

11 Princeton was a typical traditional rural community in Wisconsin, with a small-town charm feeling. Nowadays, though still small, it is known for its unique stores and restaurants. As of January 2016, the City of Princeton lists its population as 1,216.

were needed to support a household. Living with the family for whom they worked would save travel time and expenses. The eight-year age difference told me they most likely did not attend school together.

Rural families gathered to help each other out, especially during harvest time. It was common that a fall harvest activity would also become a social event, where people of all ages gathered. As described by one writer, "On crisp moonlit evenings, unmarried young people husked corn until late at night, when the host and hostess provided cider and coffee, bread and cake and sausage."[12] Maybe somewhere, in this setting or another (churches were also the centers for social life for many people) a spark was struck between Charles and Hulda. No one ever spoke of how their engagement came about and there is no one left to ask.

The eight-year age difference also puzzled me. Why had Charles, at twenty-four, not married earlier and why had he married such a young woman? In researching my question, I found that Charles' age was typical for a man's first marriage during the late 1800s.[13] Instead, it was Hulda's age that should have raised my curiosity. Her birthday was September 14; she had turned sixteen just six weeks before marrying, significantly younger than the typical age of first marriages for women in 1894, which was twenty-two.

What were the personalities of the two families that had been joined by Charles' and Hulda's marriage? What family traits, instilled in them as part of their upbringing, attracted them to each other? There were

---

12 Ernst, Kathleen, *A Settler's Year*, Madison, WI, Wisconsin Historical Society Press, 2015, p.87.

13 The U.S. Census Bureau started collecting marriage data in 1890. The average age of a first marriage for men was 26 years, and the average age of marriage for women was 22 years. Source: United States Census Bureau, People and Households, Family and Living Arrangements Main, Data, Historical Time Series, Families and Living Arrangements, Marital Status (tables) https://www.census.gov/hhes/families/files/graphics/MS-2.pdf

surely many cultural similarities that made them compatible. European immigrants of that era, and their families, had come to the United States for different reasons: religious freedom, to escape mandatory military obligations (conscription), to get away from struggles over political boundaries (wars) and the desire of financial independence. By owning property and working on it, they could significantly improve their lives.

Author Brian A. Podoll states that while researching his own paternal ancestry in Green Lake, (Princeton being in said county), "I discovered a pattern of settlement among German immigrants. This pattern indicated that the majority originated from the same vicinity of the former Prussian kingdom."[14] Confirming that statement, Charles and Hulda's families had come from the same area in Europe, shared a common history and similar dreams for their families, as many Prussian immigrants did in the township of Princeton, Wisconsin.

Even though they were coming to a new country and willing to accept changes, my ancestors - like so many others - brought with them their family traditions, habits, ways of life, culture, as well as their strong religious beliefs; attitudes that were deeply ingrained and resistant to change, even after a transatlantic move for a fresh start in the United States. In researching his own ancestry, Podoll also found that "Animosity between Polish Catholics, German Protestants and the sizable Jewish minority was commonplace but rarely violent" back in the old country. However, in the new world, that was less of a problem and immigrants, although having a tendency to cluster in enclaves with others of similar background still found it necessary to do business and work together with those of other religions. Charles' and Hulda's families were Evangelicals, a strict fundamentalist protestant group with roots in the Reformation. Once they immigrated to this country however, they were known as "German Methodists."

Two other important and intertwined reasons, drove them to come to the United States for a better life. One was the northeast European

---

14 Podoll, Brian A., C.G.R.S., *Prussian Netzelanders and Other German Immigrants in Green Lake, Marquette & Waushara Counties, Wisconsin.* Heritage Books, Inc., "Foreword."

conflicts over political boundaries; the other, the availability of land in the U.S. These motivations were equally important stimuli to migration, especially for people coming from the Prussian kingdom where country boundaries frequently changed because of wars and politics.

According to Podoll, the areas they emigrated from were "the least industrially developed provinces in Prussia, relying on agriculture farmed on sandy, marshy lowlands, like that part of Wisconsin (Green Lake County)" they came to. The immigrants who farmed in this area, as well as these two families whose children were to marry, would have found the geographic characteristics of Princeton similar to what they left behind in Prussia, with the added benefit of a more stable political environment and the economic opportunity to finally purchase land of their own.

CHAPTER 3

Vignettes on the Immigrants

Princeton Main Street, late 1800s. Courtesy Princeton Historical Society.

INTRODUCING THE BANDTS'

OF THE TWO FAMILIES, THE Bandt's immigrated to the United States in 1856. Hulda's father, Christian Friedrich (Fred) Bandt was born November 26, 1826 in the village of Schlagentin, Brandenburg, Germany which at the time was part of Prussia. He married Gustina Sauer, July 10, 1854 while still in Germany. Leaving the port of Hamburg on a sailing ship, they landed in Quebec, Canada and continued their journey to the United States in 1856, making their way to Wisconsin and finally settling in Princeton township. All this I was able to learn from The Bandt Family Genealogy Newsletter of 1987.

During their first four years in this country, Fred and Gustina bought a forty-acre plot of land a few miles southeast of Princeton, which they farmed. The same newsletter informed me that "F. Bandt built the house from stone from a quarry located on the original 40-acre plot. That lime-stone quarry, shown on the 1875 plat map, provided material for houses, barns and roadways locally and in nearby communities." Initially, Fred, Gustina and their six children lived there, and although the dwelling underwent many changes over the years, it still stands there today and is currently inhabited.

In March 1871, Gustina died leaving him with six young ones to raise. At that time, they had recently hired a live-in housekeeper, Wilhelmine (Minnie) Fausch, who had also come to this country from Germany only a few months earlier, to help with their children. Within the same month of Gustina's passing, Fred married Minnie and life went on. This second marriage was just as fruitful as his first, producing six more children, the third child being my grandmother Hulda.[15]

An 1875 plat map of Princeton township shows that by then, 19 years after arriving in the U.S, "F. Bandt" had acquired an additional 200 acres, connected to the original forty acres they had initially purchased. He was also the owner of an additional twenty-acre plot located a short distance away, which led me to believe he had prospered as a farmer and was living the lifestyle he had come to this country to pursue. Fred Bandt lived in the Princeton area for the rest of his life. He is buried in the Princeton City cemetery,

---

15 Through the same Bandt Family Newsletter I learned that in fact, Gustina and Minnie each had nine pregnancies, but only six living children each.

originally named "Westside" cemetery, along with his wives, having outlived both.

INTRODUCING THE KUEHNS'

William Kuehn, my great-grandfather on my father's side, arrived in the U.S. in 1869 and also settled in Princeton, Wisconsin. The Pedrick Genealogy Notebooks state that his future bride, Wilhelmine Fadhka, was born in Germany in 1846 and came with her parents to this country settling on a farm near Princeton.[16] I found no specific address where either of them lived after arriving in the Princeton Township area. It must have been a short time after my great grandfather William immigrated that he met and married my great grandmother because in October of 1870 they welcomed their first child, "Carl" (Charles) Kuehn, known to me as Grandpa Charly.

To my surprise, the 1870 census does not list them. Did they live and work at another landowner's farm? Did they temporarily stay with family or neighbors who also had emigrated from Prussia, so they were not individually listed? Censuses are required to record all household members and their reason for living at that address, whether they are members of the immediate family, relatives, boarders, servants, or laborers. William and Wilhelmine Kuehn do not appear in the 1870 census.

I discovered that within the next five years, more Kuehn families settled in this Princeton Township, as the 1875 plat map shows, however I'll never come to know how they were related. These Kuehn family farms were clustered around the area's German Methodist church, the same church where, later, my grandparents Charles and Hulda would marry.

---

16 Pedrick, Samuel, *Pedrick Genealogy Notebooks*, "William Kuehn." Included under the same reference is information from Wilhelmine's obituary. Census records show two different spellings of her maiden name, Fetke and Fedke.

In my research, I've never found any land ownership on Princeton plat maps for my great-grandfather William Kuehn, leading me to the conclusion that from the time he arrived in this country in 1869 and all the way up to 1894, after his first son had married, my great-grandfather had not reached a level of prosperity where he could afford (or felt ready) to buy land.

THE BURIED FACTS

Without the benefit of family stories being passed down through the years, and given that my family didn't have a public life, finding information in any type of media was difficult. There were no stories about the Kuehns' or the Bandts' in the local newspaper archives, other than obituaries or marriage announcements. My interest in their financial, social, and familial prosperity forced me to look elsewhere. The few documents I found, listed below, provided a good backbone to my grandparent's past:

* The 1860, 1870 and 1880 censuses for Princeton Township (Wisconsin) - found on the (internet) ancestry site *HeritageQuest Online and Familysearch.org*
* The 1860, 1875 and 1901 plat maps of Princeton Township (Wisconsin) found at the Dartford Historical Society archives in Green Lake, Wisconsin.
* Two tax documents for Princeton Township (Wisconsin): An "Assessment Roll of Personal Property" (1880) at the Princeton Historical Society in Princeton, Wisconsin and a fascinating document titled "Tabular Statement of Value of Lands and Agricultural Products" (1885) also located at the Dartford Historical Society in Green Lake (Wisconsin).

The censuses of 1860 and 1870 determined a family's economic status relative to their land ownership, "Value of Real Estate Owned", "Value of

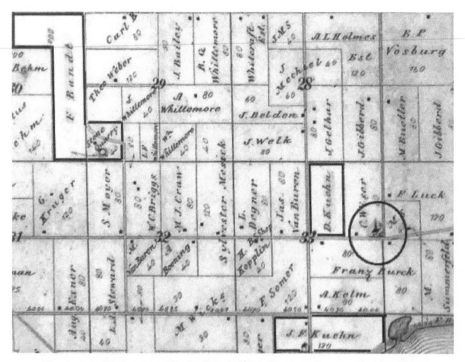

Plat map of Princeton Township, 1875, showing the location of Fred
Bandt's farm (Upper Left). There were other Kuehn families in the area
but their relationship to my great-grandfather is unknown. The German
Methodist Church symbol (Circled) is where Charles and Hulda would
later be married. Plat Map courtesy Dartford Historical Society.

Real Estate" and "Value of Personal Estate."[17] The 1860 census however
is of historical importance, as author Adam Goodheart points out that
for one, Abraham Lincoln was elected president that year, and the states
of Wisconsin and Minnesota were experiencing huge growth in populations. "Preliminary figures that began appearing as early as September
1860 confirmed what many Americans already suspected: immigration
and westward expansion were shifting the country's balance of popula-

---

17 The census of 1860 was the last US census where much of the Southern wealth included the value of slaves- still considered legal property and which showed up on these
censuses as part of the landowner's property value.

Plat map of Princeton Township, 1901, showing Fred
Bandt's farm by now having sold off 120 acres of the 200-
acre plot. Courtesy Dartford Historical Society.

tion and power... Since the last count, in 1850, the North's population
had increased 41 percent, while the South's had grown only 27 percent... The demographic prodigy was Wisconsin. Worried Southerners
could not fail to notice that the areas of the greatest population boom,
were all in the North. Wisconsin and Minnesota were of course free
states."[18] Free state meaning a state in the US in which slavery was illegal
(before the Civil War). In scrolling through the pages of data recorded
by the census enumerator in the 1860 census, Fred Bandt declared a real
estate value of $500 and personal estate property, other than real estate,
of $200 (assets located on the 40 acres he owned.)

18 Goodheart, Adam, "The census of doom," http://opinionator.blogs.nytimes.com

Ten years later, at the time of the 1870 census, his worth had grown tenfold showing now a real estate value of $5,000 (presumably the value of the additional acreage he is shown as owning on the 1875 plat map) and personal estate property, other than real estate, of $500 an increase of two hundred and fifty percent.

My great grandfather's family, William Kuehn, having not arrived in this country until 1869 is not listed on the 1860 Princeton township census, nor are they on the 1870 census (for Princeton township and surrounding areas). Local historical society aids have told me the 1870 census might have started in 1869 and my ancestors could have just been "missed" by the census taker.

It is in 1880 that my great-grandfather William Kuehn appears on an *Assessment Roll of Personal Property*. The data states he had "1 head of 'Neat' cattle" (most likely an ox or a cow), and 2 shares of bank stock for a total valuation of $15, with a note suggesting they lived in the Village of Princeton at that time. He is also listed on the 1880 *Princeton Township Census* as a farmer with a wife and six children. Not only were they able to support themselves but they had also put a little money away.

It was surprising to discover that both my great grandfathers, Fred Bandt and William Kuehn, whose families would ten years later become related through their children's marriage, appear under the column "Owner or Manager" on the 1885 *Tabular Statement of Value of Lands and Agricultural Products*. I always wondered if William was just being paid as a managing tenant farmer (which the 1880 tax document would suggest) explaining why he would not appear on a plat map as a landowner. The information clearly revealed that the Bandt family my grandfather Charles would marry into had accumulated greater wealth than his own family at that time.

After their marriage in October 1894, and before year's end, Hulda became pregnant with their first child, Frederick. His arrival was expected for the summer of 1895. What's more, in the spring of 1895, my great-grandfather, William Kuehn (Grandpa Charly's father), was finally able to purchase a farm, being able to move away from working

NAMES.	Horses No.	Val.	Neat Cattle No.	Val.	Mules and Asses No.	Val.	Sheep and Lambs No.	Val.	Swine No.	Val.	Wagons, Carriages & Sleighs No.	Val.	Watches No.	Val.	Pianos and Melodeons No.	Val.	Shares of Bank Stock No.	Val.	Value of Merchants' & Manufacturers' Stock	Value of all Personal Property	Total value of all personal prop. as aforesaid.
Schweiger August	4	150	6	50			2	12	5	10	2	30					6			40	292
Schweiger Gottlieb (31)	5	250	6	45			25	40	2	5	2	35					11			15	390
Schweiger Gustav	2	100									2	50					2		150		300
Schweiger Gottlieb (23)	1	35	2	25			2	3	8	5							2			2	70
Schweiger Wm F.	2	120	2	25			2	3	2	3	1	5					12			9	165
Schweiger John g	2	125	3	35			2	3	2	5	1	5					12			32	205
Schweiger William	2	130	6	50			5	8	2	12	2	15					12			125	340
Schweiger C A	2	120	10	89			15	20	4	10	2	20					6			2	252
Kostetak John			1	15					2	5							2				20
Stonuka John			1	15													2				15
Kuehn Wilhelm (Sen.) 2	2	100	9	65			4		4	10	1	35					1			2	202
Kuehn William (Jun.)	2	120	1	15			14	20	5	10	1	10					2			15	
Kuehn Daniel	2	120	8	65					8	6	1	10					12			50	275
Kuehn Albertine	2		2	30					2	3							12				36
King Louis	1	50	2	25					1	5	1	5		5			2		347		430

Princeton Township *Assessment Roll of Personal Property*, 1880, used for calculating taxes. The listing shows a Wilhelm and a William, Kuehn. My great-grandfather's given name was Wilhelm which he changed to William after he immigrated. My assumption is this is the same person with separate listings to differentiate his property at the farm where he "sharecropped" from the property where he "lived" in town. Notice after the name William the word "village" showing what he owned there and, after the name Wilhelm the word "Band" which may be the name Bandt with whom he may have farmed. Courtesy Princeton Historical Society.

Princeton township *Assessment Roll of Personal Property*, 1880, used for calculating taxes. The listing shows the property owned by Frederick Bandt. I believe F. Bandt and W. Kuehn sharecropped with this being Bandt's portion of the farm property. Courtesy Princeton Historical Society.

for someone else. He had established himself in the community and knew his way around, and more importantly, his sons were now old enough to help him tend to farm activities. All this was optimum growth for the Kuehn's, plus now his first grandson was on the way.

My great grandfather William found a piece of land in Metomen Township, in nearby Fond du Lac County (approximately 20 miles east of where they were living in Princeton.) The available farm could be purchased with favorable terms (negotiable) from owners E.R. and Charles Smith of Green Lake, and an agreement was reached in the spring of 1895, when he signed a promissory note as a mortgage to the current owners.

I was unable to find the negotiated price for the whole farm as the amount on the note covered only the down payment of $1,800. The entire transaction was done quickly, perhaps to allow Charles' father to take possession of, and begin operating, the farm in the spring of 1895 (giving him enough time to prepare the soil and plant, so he could harvest his first crops that same year.)

Land records show that by the fall of 1895, the note between Princeton State Bank and my great grandparents William & Wilhelmine Kuehn, had been satisfied. The data also shows them as residing in Metomen Township now, meaning he had moved his family to the farm that previous spring.

My great-grandfather was 53 years old when he purchased the farm in 1895. Keeping in mind the life expectancy in the U.S. for an adult male at that time was 45.2 years, he must have decided this farm would be his legacy, the opportunity for financial stability he could offer to all his seven children.

CHAPTER 4

The Making of a Family

Main Street, Brandon, the largest community in Metomen township, circa 1900. The Brandon Times, image courtesy of the Brandon Historical Society.

MY GRANDFATHER'S EXPRESSION ON HIS wedding photo confused me. Was he content and hiding a smile? Was his gaze steady because he was performing a duty, something expected of him? At times I tell myself his look is saying *I'm ready to be a man and support a family.* We know that smiling was not common in the 1800s. Because photography evolved from portraiture, where people sat for long hours, making it impossible to hold a smile for so long. As artist and writer Nicholas Jeeves points out, "Smiling also has a large number of discrete cultural and histori-cal significances, few of them in line with our modern perceptions of it being a physical signal of warmth, enjoyment, or indeed of happiness. By the 17th century in Europe it was a well-established fact that the only people who smiled broadly, in life and in art, were the poor, the lewd, the drunk, the innocent, and the entertainment".

I imagine my grandparents' wedding was a nice, simple, and traditional German ceremony. Not only could he be proud of starting a married life, but now my grandfather had a great opportunity at his hands. His father was purchasing a farm for the family, where he and his brothers could put his skills to good use. With commitment, dedication, hard work and good fortune, they could all prosper. And since my great grandfather, had already been managing a farm in Princeton township for many years, he could easily run a fully equipped farm of his own.

Speculation is that Charles and Hulda lived with her parents, the Bandt's, from the autumn when they married until the following sum-mer - at which time the Kuehn farm was up and running. When putting myself in my grandfather's shoes, the question I most pondered was: Was living with his in-laws an obstacle to proving his worthiness in the eyes of his new wife and her family?

There is an old tongue-in-cheek saying about newlyweds, "*the first child can come anytime*," and as things turned out, their first child was born in Princeton nine months after their wedding day, with a birth date recorded as July 28, 1895.[19] Following tradition, my grandparents hon-

---

19 Births were not always recorded, especially for rural families and if the child was born at home. Families were too busy with farm work to make it into the city to register the new child. The birthdate used here was obtained from Fred's 1917 World War I draft registration. **Note:** In 1852, Wisconsin directed its counties to record births, a man-date generally ignored. In 1878, a similar law received more attention and adherence. However, it was 1907 before the State Bureau of Vital Statistics was established to collect all this information. Source: www.genealoger.com/wisconsin/wi_vital_records.htm.

ored both their fathers by naming the baby Fredrick Wilhelm Kuehn. "Uncle Fred", as I would come to know him.

Discovering Metomen and the Surrounding Areas

Though officially located within Fond du Lac County, geographically Metomen is a quiet township southeast of community of Green Lake and south of the city of Ripon, with undulating prairies, marshes, and groves of heavy forests. Its name means "grain of corn" or "ground corn" in the Menominee language. Settlers arrived in this fertile territory in 1844 and 1845, claiming all the government lands available in just those two years. Local citizens organized and named Metomen in 1846, at a house meeting of resident F.D. Bowman. The villages of Fairwater and Brandon were considered part of the township as well. Historical records state farmers sought property here because of its sandy loam, subsoil of gravel, and occasional limestone deposits. The richness also came from three small waterways which nourished the area as well: The east branch of the Rock River, the Grand River and a large spring that fed Silver Creek (which to this day empties into Green Lake). The lowlands, when drained, were warm and abundant with vegetable mold[20] which for those working the land, equated to significant agricultural wealth. By the time my great grandfather purchased the farm, fifty years after Metomen had formed, the area was well established and bustling with activity. The 1885 Wisconsin census for Metomen Township listed 1,359 total residents, of which 704 were males and 655 females.

My great grandpa William and his family were already living at the new Metomen farm by the time Charles and Hulda arrived and rented a house near an important area crossroads community called "Reeds Corners."

---

20 Vegetable mold is present in soils that are rich in humus. Like leaf mold or compost.

When I think of Metomen and Reeds Corners, I remember visiting my grandparents at one time and overhearing their conversations, commenting about having proudly lived near "Reed's Corners." This intersection had become a self-made community, taking its name from landowner Warren Reed. Mr. Reed's extensive farm and land holdings surrounded the crossing of two roads between Ripon and Brandon. This corner was an important interaction point in the area, allowing both locals and travellers to share stories, learn news, stop for a rest, get something to eat or purchase goods. Reed's Corners housed the first area post office (1852) and train depot (1856), a few general stores where one could purchase groceries, farm products and tools, and two churches (a Wesleyan, later Congregational church, and a Methodist church). Nearby, the first public school of the area was erected, a saw mill was opened (1846), and the Dakin & Lathrop flour mill was built on the Grand River branch, within the nearby Village of Fairwater (1847).

Today, only the Bethel Cemetery remains to pin the location of Reed's Corners and what used to be an area of commercial prominence. The farmlands surrounding it no longer tell the stories of the families who built their lives there, laying the foundation for their future generations.

Holmes School was of particular interest to me. This would have been the one-room country schoolhouse their first four children attended. Though I have found abundant area information about the land, life, people, and places that surrounded my grandparents, I am still left to wonder exactly where their first house was. It's a closure I'd like to have, but that now seems impossible. Life plays a mean joke, making us become interested in our personal heritage when it's long gone and there are few people, if anyone, left to ask.

Even though these towns and villages continue to be there today, and seem to have changed so little, the areas they are in, *have* changed. Few buildings remain with their original architecture, but the geographical landscapes and histories have significantly evolved, making the past of such a small place at times seem unrecognizable. Metomen, has also

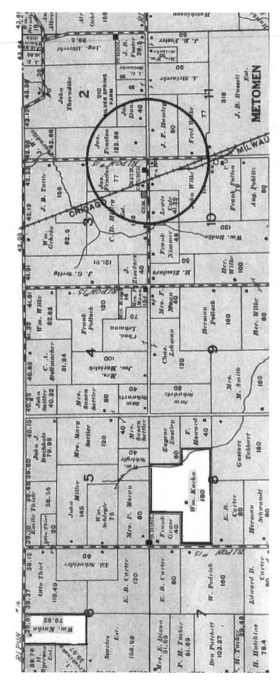

Portion of the 1910 plat map of Metomen township showing the location of the farm and land owned by my great-grandfather William Kuehn (Outlined) from 1895 until 1920 and its proximity to Reeds Corners (Circle). Courtesy Brandon Historical Society.

withstood the wear of time and civilization. Though still rural, and an agricultural community, it no longer showcases the lush forests the settlers once talked about finding there.

The Metomen area was also home to the famous and prosperous Utley Quarry, a populous and almost self-sustaining village. Utley Quarry, named after Charles P. Utley, offered a unique type of granite[21] called rhyolite. A community of about 250 people made up the village of Utley surrounding the quarry in the middle-to-late 19th century. C.P. Utley, and others, convinced the railroad to build a spur line to transport granite to Milwaukee and Chicago where it was used for cobblestones to pave streets, construct buildings and as water breaks along the shore of Lake Michigan.

The railroad still passes through to haul out aggregate, with the land and quarry now privately owned, but none of the successful area developments (Utley Quarry, Reed's Corners, flour mills, or even the train depots) would stand the test of time and industrial change that was coming.

---

21 Geologists believe the hill was created by an outflow of lava eons ago resulting in unusually hard granite, black in color. The lava which created the rock is an "inlier" found in an unusual knob shaped hill that stood, looking out of place, in the Grand River valley, that cropped up through the surrounding Paleozoic sedimentary rocks. Utley village, now considered a ghost town, is located between the community of Fairwater, in Metomen township and the community of Markesan, in Green Lake township.

CHAPTER 5

The Road Ahead

A scene similar to what Charles and Hulda saw as they were leaving
Princeton to their new home in Metomen. Drawing from "The
Call of the Open Road" compiled by the Wisconsin Advancement
Association and printed by the Milwaukee Journal.

THE HIGHLIGHT OF THE SUMMER of 1895 for Grandpa Charles, Hulda and baby Friedrich was the move from Hulda's parents to their new rented home. Surely a step in the right direction towards independence and self-sufficiency.

In the late 1800s, local travel in rural Wisconsin was still done by a horse drawn wagon with few personal belongings packed away in trunks. The dirt and gravel roads from Princeton to Metomen were a rough ride to endure with an infant. In perfect road conditions, a coach driven by a fresh team of horses could "cut dirt" at the pace of nine miles per hour.[22]

Using two local plat maps, I plotted the route Grandpa must have chosen to take from the Bandt's farm in Princeton to arrive in Metomen, and estimated they traveled approximately twenty miles to get there. On a good day, with optimum weather conditions, what today is considered a short trip, probably took them up to six hours to complete at an even four or five miles per hour pace.

Many times I've put myself in Grandpa's shoes, especially when thinking about and recreating his trip to Metomen. I've speculated what thoughts crossed his mind in anticipation of traveling to their new home. I remember the anxiety and partial fear of when I left my parents' house to join the Army. I can't imagine what it must have been like for Grandpa to leave on a horse drawn wagon to a new house, with a new wife and baby, travelling on their own through dirt rural roads. Although there are no recorded facts about this trip within my family, his voice and actions resonate in my head, as if he's telling me the story himself, as if making the trip myself.

Hulda and Mrs. Bandt made preparations for traveling with the baby. He needed blankets to lie in when Hulda wasn't holding or feeding him. I hoped the steady plodding of the horse's hooves and the wagon swaying will lull baby Fred to sleep...

Theirs was probably a single horse drawn wagon, the kind used for hauling light loads around on the farm. Those farm wagons were merely

---

22 From *The Writer's Guide to Everyday Life in the 1800s* by Marc McCutcheon, pg. 53.

a wooden box, four feet wide and ten feet long with side and end boards two feet high. The box more than likely was set directly on the axles of the wagon running gear and did not have a spring suspension. It would be a jarring ride as the wrought iron wheels rolled along over any ruts and bumps on the gravel road.

The driver's seat was mounted near the front on the box of the wagon. The seating part simply a board with a burlap bag filled with straw or a folded horse blanket, if anything at all.

I picked up extra feed the day before so Chief was well fed before we left. He could graze in the prairie when we stopped for lunch. I brought along extra hay to put in the bottom of the wagon box, underneath the blankets, to cushion Fred's bed. Dietmar had come by the farm to see that Chief was properly shod. I'd made sure the wagon Mr. Bandt had lent me was ready to go; I had greased the wheels and tightened the lock nuts. I sure didn't want the wheels to fall off! It wasn't an elegant carriage, or prairie schooner, but it would get us there. Chief's harness was good and didn't need repairs. Hulda packed our clothes in the trunks mother had given us. I can't forget the water jugs. Two? Three? Two should be enough. I'll fill them from the well early in the morning just before we leave and put them under the seat, in the shade with some hay packed around them for insulation. In the Bandt's shanty, I set aside some candles, cleaned the soot off two kerosene lamps and the large iron kettle, the one that belonged to Mrs. Minnie's family, that she said we could take. Hulda would pack our chamber set and toiletries. Father hadn't been specific on what furnishings we would find in the house he rented for us, but whatever pieces of furniture we didn't have, I could make. We knew there was at least a cord[23] of leftover wood at the property that would help get us by until I could restock it. Hulda said she'd refill our mattress with straw once we got to our new home. I sure did hope the house had a spring bed bottom and not rope.

With preparations completed and the day to move having arrived, Grandpa must have awakened in the thin of that summer morning feeling a mixture of excitement and tension.

---

23 A cord of wood is a stack 8'x8'x4'. Back then a family needed at least ten cords to get through the winter.

When we set out to our new home I knew father and Mr. Bandt would be proud. The weather that morning didn't seem as if it would be a problem, it didn't look as if it was going to rain.[24] We would travel well. While Hulda finished up in the house and got baby Fred ready I asked her brother Otto, to help me get the horse harnessed and hitched to the wagon. I was hoping the trails wouldn't be too dusty to move by hoof.

The trunks and other belongings would have been loaded into the wagon with the help of Grandma Hulda's family members, especially her father and brothers if they weren't working at the family farm or quarry. The food basket most likely included liver sausage, a loaf of bread, cheese, sorghum syrup, and maybe some huckleberries or fruits off the property.

When I thought we were all loaded up, it was time to say our "goodbyes." Mrs. Minnie was holding little Fred and had tears in her eyes that she dried with her kitchen apron. I could tell she was happy for us, for Hulda of course, but also very sad we were leaving.

I helped Hulda onto the wagon and then Mrs. Bandt handed her the baby. Fred, being only a few weeks old, was warmly dressed and covered up for our long ride out. His left hand gripped a small rag doll, one Hulda had made for him when he was born. When I took my seat, I noticed Hulda looked sad. Taking her hand, I told her it was time to go. There was no need for tears, we wouldn't be that far away.

With a quick click of the tongue and lift of the reins, Chief moved along forward. Hulda and I looked back for a long time at the Bandt's house and farm-stead where we had met, lived, and worked since marrying.

I felt happy and grateful waving to our family members standing outside. As if he knew we would remember this day forever, Chief walked at a slow pace, pulling the wagon down the driveway past the barns and out onto the graveled road.[25]

---

24 According to the Wisconsin State Climatology Office archives records show the year of 1895 was about average in temperature but was the driest year on record for the next decade and beyond. www.aos.wisc.edu. However, rural Wisconsin is known for impromptu heavy summer storms that can last a few minutes then quickly go away.

25 In 1895, there was still no scheme developed to identify roads, so none of these roads had been assigned any names, numbers, or letters. Those living and familiar with the area knew which roads to take, but for others, they would need to depend on the locals' verbal directions or look for signs attached to fence posts or buildings at the

This picture (circa 1890), although not of the Bandt family, is reminiscent of what Charles and Hulda may have seen when they departed the Bandt farm. Courtesy Princeton Historical Society.

We had a dog named Hans back then and he was excited to be going along with us; his presence was a welcomed company.

We were on our own now and I knew the way. I'd been on those roads before when I helped Pa move to the new farm. I hoped the trip wouldn't be too hard on Hulda and the baby. To think that the gravel on the road we traveled came from Mr. Bandt's quarry. Little did he imagine that one day all his hard work would also pave the path to our future.

We made a right turn at the end of the driveway, starting our way up and around the hill. The climb seemed to take longer than I had calculated and we'd not even gone half a mile. After topping the hill and going around the bend, we headed straight south, the road gradually sloping downhill. Chief seemed to brace himself a bit, so I kept the reins tight when the load felt like it could be too much for him. After about half a mile, we came to an intersection where we turned east

intersections that may have been constructed to point out directions or had painted on them mileage to a destination.

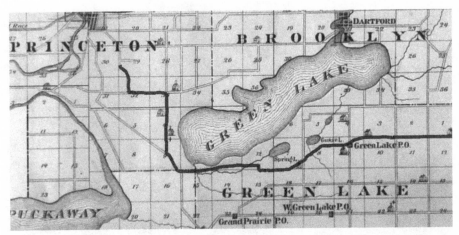

The heavy black line is the route I believe Charles, Hulda
and baby Fred traveled from Princeton to Metomen.
Map courtesy Dartford Historical Society

*again. After another rugged country mile, at the next intersection we turned right
and kept heading south, past the west end of Green Lake.*

*We continued due south with the road leveling out as we traveled through
the rolling farmland; it was easy for Chief to pull the wagon. There hadn't been
much to see in that stretch except farm fields, other farmsteads, the one room
schoolhouse, and a church. In the distant hills northwards was the glacial valley
that holds the waters of Big Green Lake. Neighbors and friends would go to the
lake on Sundays after service for a family picnic. On hot summer days they'd walk
barefoot along the sandy edge of the lake to refresh themselves in the cool water.
We'd only done that on few occasions. By the time we returned home from church,
had dinner, then rode to the lake, there wasn't much time to enjoy the water as we
had to get back home for evening chores.*

*If we didn't have such a long stretch ahead of us that day I would have liked
to stop there for a short break. Hulda was still quiet, but a small smile now seemed
to rise in her face. In my heart I knew she was happy for us. She continually looked
around, admiring the changing landscapes which told me she was enjoying the
trip. When a flock of wild turkeys crossed the road in front of us causing Hans to*

wake up and start barking, she laughed. Baby Fred never noticed the commotion, and napped away in the back.

I showed Hulda how we were rounding the southwest portion of the lake... that was about where the dividing line between Princeton and Green Lake was. The locals called it "The Terrace." As the lake came into view I guided Chief near a feeding stream so he could get himself some water. When he had his fill, we kept going, crossing the small bridge over the creek, now headed due east, following the south shoreline. Green Lake was so beautiful in the summer.

From my place in the wagon I could see the hills we still had to traverse. Those hills, I would find out later, were part of the sheer bluffs that form the lake shoreline. I knew traveling up those hills was probably going to be the most difficult part of the journey. It was a long, steep climb and the ride would be slow going.

After riding for almost two hours, my grandfather would still be taking it all in, not only because it was a journey he'd want to remember, but also because his family was waiting for them in Metomen and would probably ask about the trip.

At the next ample and dry clearing by the road, we gave ourselves a respite and got off the wagon to stretch our legs, relieve ourselves and feed the baby. It was a good place for Chief to graze and gather some strength before the climb we had ahead. How nice it was to be alone in the countryside, hearing the sounds of summer and enjoying the scenery. We were quite hungry by then, so while Hulda changed and fed little Fred, I made ourselves a plate of Braunschweiger, cheese and bread. The picnic basket was full of treats Mrs. Bandt had prepared for us. God bless her soul, that woman always took such good care of us.

With each mile we traveled, I continued to think about how it had taken us weeks to prepare for this trip, so much ruckus for twenty miles. To think Mama and Papa left Posen on a transatlantic ship bound for America with just enough money to pay for their journey, and now Papa had bought a farm and was a landowner. Better yet, William Jr., Henry and myself can work the farm with him as well. We Kuehns finally have something to our name in America.

We finished our picnic and took a quick rest, after which we had to get back on the road if we wanted to make it to Metomen before sunset. When Chief was ready and everyone settled in the wagon, we started off. Fred was a bit fussy, but quickly fell asleep with the swaying ride. When we got to where the road began the uphill climb, I noticed the steep gravel road bed hadn't been graded well and had deep ruts from other wagon wheels, made even worse by the erosion from the recent spring rains. Realizing it would be difficult enough for Chief to pull our loaded wagon I decided to hop off and walk for a while and see how we fared. I told Hulda she and the baby would be safer if she held him close.

After loosely fastening the reins I climbed down next to Chief and walked, leading him up the hill. Hans followed along right next to me, eager to guard our journey and keep me company.

They were now about halfway there. After reaching the high point in the road, the land leveled out for the next several miles as they traveled past fields of wheat, oats and barley that were cut, shocked and ready for threshing; and corn that was now in the tassel stage. Their journey continued through a community at a crossroads where there was a church, a cemetery, a school, and a post office, known today as the intersection of County Road K and County Road N (a restaurant named Center House occupies that corner these days).

The surroundings looked somewhat different than the landscape they knew growing up in the countryside around Princeton. In front of them was more prairie-like terrain, rich shades of green and yellow painting the rural landscape. A few more miles onward, they would cross the dividing line between Green Lake and Fond du Lac counties, entering at last Metomen Township.

Grandpa Charles, grandma Hulda and uncle Fredrick were almost home.

CHAPTER 6

Metomen Becomes Home

My grandfather with his family, circa 1890. Back row from left to right: Siblings Marie, William Jr., Minnie, Henry, and Edith. Front row from left to right: My grandfather Charles, his mother Wilhelmine, father William Sr. and sister Louise. Kuehn Family Collection.

By late afternoon or early evening, the journey would have been over, and Grandpa Charles would have steered the wagon, with all their belongings, onto the dirt path leading to the rented house near Reeds Corners.

I visited the local historical societies in the nearby towns (Fairwater, Brandon, Markesan, Princeton, Green Lake, Ripon, and Berlin), to become familiar with room layouts, kitchen arrangements, everyday utensils, and ways-of-life. A walk through the small towns of Brandon and Fairwater gave me a sense of space, direction and of wonder: What did these roads, sidewalks and buildings look like back then? I found myself speculating, gazing into the past, into what Grandpa Charles must have seen and felt when they rolled across their new property lines.

It had been a long day. I was tired and Hulda was too. A great sense of pride and relief washed over me. Pa, William, and Henry were waiting for us on the porch. They looked more beat and grimy than we did even after being on the road all day. I could tell by their clothes they had been working the fields and hadn't yet washed up.

When we stepped down from the wagon, Ma and my younger sister Minnie came out of the house to greet us. They were excited to see us, but most of all, to hold baby Fred. Ma said Mrs. Vande Berg, our new landlady, had opened the house for her so she could get it ready. Hans was so excited, he wouldn't stop running around and barking at everyone, even waking up Fred who by now had started squalling. Our arrival had created quite a commotion in what was otherwise a quiet evening in the Brandon countryside.

Before we unloaded the wagon, we took a quick look inside. Of course, we were grateful to see this place that was going to be our new home. Stepping into the house gave me a feeling of relief mixed with exhaustion. I didn't want Hulda to be disappointed, but it was what we could afford and we wouldn't have to live with either of our families.

The kitchen had a cooking range, blackened by years of use, a yellowed wooden table with a couple of chairs, and an indoor hand pump over the single basin sink. This was good news - it meant there was a cistern under the house we could use for washing up - we'd only have to fetch water from the outdoor well for drinking and cooking then. Ma pointed to the icebox in the corner and said it needed to be cleaned, the hinges were rusty and it needed new ones, but for now it would make do.

The sitting room was small but had a picture window that overlooked the front yard. From there you could see the driveway and a small section of the road we came on. Mrs. Vande Berg, a widow who had gone to live with her sister, had left us a green settee - a bit threadbare - and a wooden rocking chair which sat alone in a corner. I recognized one of Ma's knitted blankets draped over the back-rest. A large rug covered up almost the whole floor. By the looks of it, it must have been quite nice at one time.

The sleeping room was upstairs. A decent room with a bed, a dresser, a ward-robe[26] and a window that faced the back of the lot, mostly overlooking the trees, the outhouse and the neighbor's field. Not bad. We could put the baby's crib in the corner, away from the draft from the door and window. One of mother's white doilies laid on the dresser. I could tell she'd dusted the room already to make us feel at home.

Ma called to say supper was ready. The lot of us ate outside on a makeshift table and benches under the umbrella of a thick shagbark hickory tree. Ma had outdone herself with the kohlrouladen, kraut and potato salad. It was delicious and just what we needed. Our first homemade meal in Metomen. I'll never forget that dinner.

Before everyone left, William, Henry and Pa helped me unload the wagon and bring everything inside. As soon as they were gone, I unhitched Chief and put him in the barn while Hulda prepared our room. The firewood in the wood box looked good and dry, so I brought more in for the next morning. Hans was already asleep in the kitchen corner. Though he was a tough little fellow, he was beat from running next to the wagon for most of the day. This surely had been an adventure for him too.

---

26 Built in wall closets, as we know them today, were included in new house constructions in the US only after WWII, because the average American family had few possessions. However, some houses built by property developers did have closets if the property owner could afford to pay the additional tax (closets were taxed as an additional bedroom).

Sitting on the porch stoop before going to bed, I took in my surroundings. Short loud trills of gray tree frogs filled the air. The warm summer breeze had cleared the sky and all the stars were out looking down upon us. I took this as a blessing.

It shouldn't take long for us to get settled in.

It was good to be home.

WE WILL BECOME SELF-MADE MEN

Grandpa Charly, and his two brothers, now helped operate the 180-acre farm their father had purchased, plus an additional 80 acres a short distance away. Grandpa could now help with that year's harvest, especially since he hadn't been around to work with them that year during the spring and the first part of the summer.

The farm purchase was "lock, stock and barrel", meaning it included all the personal property found on it: 7 horses, 2 colts, 22 cows, 4 spring calves, 14 sheep and 25 hogs. The recording stated, in addition to the land and buildings, other assets such as farm tools, implements, wagons, carriages, cutter sleighs, harnesses, and all household furnishings. Just as important were any on-site harvested crops, which for William Sr. meant getting 200 bushels of barley, 500 bushels of oats, 600 baskets of corn (for feed) and 65 bushels of wheat.

That first spring on the farm had been busy as they became acquainted with the soil, the existing tools, and new animals around them. There was plenty of work for everyone. Even before the snow melted, and the frost was out of the ground, they had to prepare the fields for spring planting. Farming in Metomen would be an adjustment, the land was different than the soil they were used to handling in Princeton where there was less topsoil and an underlying layer of gravel provided better drainage, allowing the earth to dry and warm earlier in the year, so planting could begin sooner.

In Metomen however, the soil was heavier because of a deeper layer of topsoil on a clay base, preventing frost from exiting the ground as quickly, and for the land to dry and warm up as was needed when seeding. While waiting to get into the fields, they had to decide which crops to plant and in what sections. If the land for small grain crops (barley, oats, and wheat) hadn't been plowed the previous fall that would be the first work to get done as soon as the ground was ready (without frost). Using the horses, he could haul out and spread the manure from the piles that had accumulated during the winter, enriching the soil naturally.

They also needed to check each horse harness, make sure the farm implements were suitable for work or repaired, to avoid any one thing that could delay spring planting. Cleaning the small grain seed was necessary as well, which they did by running it through a fanning mill.[27] This time frame was also used to ready the corn by selecting and shelling ears which could be used for seed kernels. In those days farmers saved the best grains from the previous summer's harvest for sowing the following spring. Once the small grains were in the soil they could immediately begin preparing to plant corn.

Spring planting just added to what was already a busy time on the farm. Once the long Wisconsin winter was over, daily responsibilities were shared by all in order to keep the household productive and running smoothly. Everyone worked from before sunrise until sundown, hauling chopped wood to kindle the stoves, feeding and caring for livestock, milking the cows, collecting eggs, tending to the vegetable garden, cleaning the barns and stalls, as well as picking up supplies and checking the tools that were needed for next day's work. Everything needed to be done in a timely manner during the spring and summer to ensure a successful planting and harvest season. Once the first autumn

---

27 Hand operated machine driving a fan to blow out the chaff while the grain sifts through screens to remove foreign particles, leaving then only the best kernels for planting. Fanning mills were first invented around 1880 to remove the chaff from wheat used for making flour but were later also used to clean seed grains of wheat, oats, and barley before planting. http://www.farmcollector.com/equipment/fanningmill

frosts arrived, usually at the end of October, the farming year was practically over. And what they had harvested that year, was the bounty that would get them through the longer winter to come.

It would take exactly twelve months after signing a Promissory Note for my Great Grandfather William Kuehn Sr. to proudly own his farm. He was fifty-four years old at the time, and twenty-five years had passed since immigrating from Prussia to the United States.

Because the Metomen farm had more fertile land, it could produce crop yields greater than those of the farms they had operated in Princeton. Any excess crops could always be sold and used wisely. The "History of Fond du Lac County" says about one Metomen farmer's crop yield: "...in 1853, planted fifty acres of corn, hoed it but once, during the season, and harvested 3,750 bushels from it, being an average of seventy-five bushels to the acre. He sowed about twenty-five acres of wheat, from which he harvested eight hundred bushels... In 1853, a large number of the farmers, received for the surplus products of their farms, sums ranging from $1,000 to $1,800. The surplus products of the Town (Metomen), that year, are estimated to exceed $100,000."

My grandparent's marriage, the move to Metomen, and the new living arrangement must have all been working out agreeably. The new farm, now going on two years was also very productive, benefiting the whole family. Grandpa Carley must have felt confident. He had job security, a good and hardworking wife, and a comfortable home. In August of 1897, my grandparents welcomed my uncle Walter Kuehn into the family. Uncle Fredrick, now two years old, was no longer an only child. He had someone to play and roam around the farm with.

CHAPTER 7

The Ending and Beginning of a Century

Written in pencil on the back of this photo is: "Fred, Agnes, Walter -
Brandon (WI) 1902." Notice the staging of the photo with the flower
painting on the left (not hanging but leaning against a chair), and what
we believe is my grandparent's marriage certificate on the right. The
children are dressed in their Sunday attire. Kuehn Family Collection.

THE STROKE OF MIDNIGHT OF December 31, 1899 brought to a close the exciting nineteenth century. Groundbreaking historic events would propel the new century into an even more industrious era. The parting 1800s had welcomed the incredible *Expedition to The West* by Lewis & Clark (1804), the first locomotive with a steam powered engine (Stephenson, 1814) and the Erie Canal, which when completed in 1825 provided a more direct and efficient eastbound route for farm products and raw material from the "new" west (now the Midwest) to the eastern coast markets. The canal also allowed for significant western movement of manufactured products from the East Coast inland and, more importantly, the transportation of immigrants, thus aiding in the socio-economic development of the United States.

The same century saw in our country the passing of the Homestead Act[28] (1862) and the Abolition of Slavery (1865). It also introduced the invention of the telephone (Bell, 1875), the phonograph and the lightbulb (both by Edison, 1878 and 1879 respectively), the first handheld camera (Kodak, 1888) and the telegraph (Marconi, 1895). However, it would take a long time for some of these incredible inventions to make it into the houses of the rural folks of Wisconsin, and Midwest America.

From a political standpoint, the U.S. lived through and saw the consequences of the American Civil War (1861-1865), the Massacre at Wounded Knee (1890), the dedication and unveiling of the Statue of Liberty on Ellis Island (1892) and the Spanish-American War (in which the US attacked Spanish possessions in the Pacific, and gained control of Cuba, Puerto Rico, and the Philippines). How many events with world-wide effects were packed into just one hundred years. And so many more, just as significant as those, would come to revolutionize the new century.

The beginning of the 1900s, was becoming an exciting time for Grandpa Charles and Grandma Hulda. A few days into January of the new year, Hulda gave birth to their first daughter, my aunt Agnes. Frederick, four, and Walter, two, now had a sister to look after.

---

28 President Lincoln signed The Homestead Act which encouraged Western migration by providing settlers 160 acres of public land. In exchange, homesteaders paid a small filing fee and were required to complete five years of continuous residence before receiving ownership of the land.

The same year aunt Agnes was born, the Code of Law of the United States of America, required that a federal census be taken. The records for that year, 1900, list my grandparents and their three children as renting a house on farm within Metomen township.

Two more years would pass working at the Kuehn family farm when in February 1902 Grandma delivered a new family member, their third son, Benjamin. They now had four children. If their first child, uncle Fred had not been planned it certainly appears the later children had birthdays fairly evenly spaced, one child about every two years.

Four children were not an unusual family size for that time, especially for an Evangelical family who in their religious upbringing were told to "Be fruitful and multiply..." The church didn't impart guidelines for what was expected as an ideal number of children. Parents were left to decide what the minimum number was for an Evangelical family in good standing and, conversely, how many children they could afford to support.[29]

From mid-1895 until the birth of Benjamin in early 1902, the only recorded events, under my family's, name were the births of the first four children. There are no other anecdotes or stories about my family I could unearth for that time. I found myself thinking that most rural families did not make newspaper headlines back then, and did not have what most consider a "noteworthy life" - assumptions based on what *today* we would consider important. These first-generation Americans didn't have East Coast last names, a pedigree that would have made them notable. They didn't really have local family legacies to draw upon, or university educations that could have furthered their careers and led to great discoveries. *Most* immigrant families didn't own land until later in life, or never had reverberating

---

29 Census statistics between the late 1800s into the early 1900s show six member households were approximately 10 percent of the U. S. population with larger households, seven or more members, being over 20 percent. This was not necessarily the number of families containing two parents and their children because households were counted as the number of people who lived at a given address. *Historical Statistics of the United States: Colonial Times to 1970, Part 1 (Bureau of the Census, 1975), p. 42.*

Walter, Agnes, Frederick, and Benjamin, Metomen circa 1905. Walter
and Frederick are each holding a rabbit, and Agnes a pigeon. This
coupled with the flower vase in the middle, the flowered blanket
below them, and the flowers in Ben's hands suggests the picture was
taken during the spring, at Easter. Kuehn Family Collection.

accomplishments of which to boast publicly of. The few that did, were few
and far in between. It seems that very little of their rural lives made a "public" dent in the local history[30], even if so many of us relied on their efforts.
They were hard working immigrant farmers and families, who saw themselves as average people, doing what was right, making a living to survive
and propel their next family generation further. These were hard working

---

30 The Berlin Historical Society has material on patents and inventions from Berlin residents around the time Grandpa Charly was alive. A few, but not all, are: G.H. Landgraph
invented a secret telegraph sounder in 1898; Tim Fortnum developed a one-cylinder
gasoline engine for farm and marine use in 1903; Frank Chapman a blancher for food
preservation in 1926. All of these inventions are patented and can be found online.)

immigrant farmers and families, and there were so many of them, but at the end of day, they considered themselves average citizens, making a living to survive and propel their next generation further.

Community happenings did get reported in the local papers, and some are quite entertaining. But most residents weren't mentioned in the local newspapers, newsletters or history books that came later. Unless you were wealthy, involved in an accident, you passed away, committed a crime, or were getting married - or had enough money to place an ad for your business - you weren't going to be found in the local media. These dignified, quiet, and unassuming lives have left descendants like me with little to work off of, and so much to imagine and hypothesize about. Combing through files, photos, books and binders at historical societies, local libraries and government offices can be a daunting task, but I did so with the hope of turning up something new about my family I didn't know existed. For some of us, it's how we find closure.

By 1907 Fredrick was twelve, Walter, ten, Agnes, seven and Benjamin had turned five. My grandparents seemed to have had a good thing going so far, but the reality was also that they were getting older. At 37 years of age, it may have crossed my grandfather's mind he was nearing life expectancy for that time, a frightening thought for most.[31] Working the farm was arduous and sooner or later his body wouldn't be strong enough to keep up with such exertion.

In the summer of 1907, while still living in Metomen, a land contract document found among other historical family memorabilia shows that Grandpa Charly purchased a small farm of his own, made of two adjacent lots, in the southwest part of Ripon. The five acres they bought were located on the corner of Griswold and Thomas streets.

This would come to be my Grandpa Charly's farm.

---

31 Male life expectancy in 1907 was about 45 years of age. www.demog.berkeley.edu, however the data does not state if these numbers may also have applied to farmers or men working in rural communities.

CHAPTER 8

Grandma Hulda Bandt Kuehn

Grandma Hulda standing on the south side of the lawn near the garden
at the Ripon farmstead, circa mid-1930s. Kuehn Family Collection.

I DON'T RECALL MUCH ABOUT my grandmother Hulda from my early years.
She was always "there" when we'd go visit her on the farm in Ripon, and

I didn't interact with her as much as I did with Grandpa Charly. In our family, each generation stayed within its group. Back then "children were to be seen and not heard." We didn't cross those boundaries unless specifically asked to. We were just part of the family, and everyone appeared to know where they fit in.

This lack of interaction was also reinforced by her personality, because Grandma Hulda was always stern in my perception as a youngster. We were taught to treat our elders with respect, which wasn't hard to do around her because of her serious nature. Looking back now, with years of experience and an adult life lived, her demeanor may have been the result of her deteriorating health and her difficulty in getting around by the time my memories of her were cemented. That, or her inherited Prussian genes, had shaped her strong personality.

My grandmother was born Hulda Theresa Bandt on September 14, 1878, to Friedrich and Wilhelmine Bandt on their farm in rural Princeton, Wisconsin. She was the ninth of twelve children.

The Bandt Family Genealogy Archives show that my great-grandfather Christian Fredrich (Fred) Bandt (b.1826) married Gustina Sauer (b. 1830) on July 10, 1854 in their native Germany. They immigrated to the United States in 1856, settling on a small farm within two miles of the village of Princeton, Wisconsin. Their marriage produced six children between the ages of three and fifteen, when Gustina died on March 2nd, 1871.

After her passing, and within the same month, on March 31st, 1871, my great-grandfather married Wilhelmine "Minnie" Fausch (from Wirsitz, Germany, b. 1847) who had come to the United States earlier that same year to work as hired help for the Bandt family. Fred was twenty-one years her senior. It is apparent, after consulting with local historical societies, that at that time it would have been impossible for an unmarried woman to continue living in that house as her reputation would have been marred, explaining perhaps one of the reasons why the marriage most likely occurred and so quickly.

With Minnie, Fred would father six more children, of which Hulda was the third from the new marriage.

Looking out over what was Fred Bandt's land. Landscape Hulda would have seen while growing up on her family's farm. Princeton, Wisconsin.

Artist's drawing of the house in which Hulda was born.
Photo courtesy Kuehn Family Collection.

After grandma Hulda turned sixteen, she married my grandfather, and over the years brought nine children into this world. After having Frederick, Walter, Agnes and Benjamin, my father Clarence, was their fifth child after a six-year hiatus, and the first to be born after moving to their Ripon farm.

Although my grandparents were born in the U.S., they were undoubtedly influenced by their parents' way of thinking regarding customs brought with them as Prussian immigrants. In "The History of Wisconsin," John D. Buenker wrote "Of all immigrant institutions, none proved more enduring or crucial than the family. In nearly all southern and eastern European countries, the nuclear family was the principal tool for organizing how lives were led, determining patterns for socialization, and distributing land and other resources... Parents decided careers and marriage partners, determined whether children should work or attend school, and provided job training... A married woman with children generally managed the household..."[32]

Grandma Hulda was a strong woman who did everything in the home, fulfilling the role of family matriarch to every extent, and for as long as I can remember. As such, it was her position to give out orders. Always.

I clearly remember one of those simple yet very specific directives. It was a summer weekend morning when my brother Carl and I were visiting them. We were about to go to the barnyard to watch Grandpa Charly feed the animals, when she turned from what she was doing in the kitchen and said to him in a stern tone *"Make sure you watch over the kids so they don't get hurt."* I recall those words like if she had said them today. Because of her tone, it was clear that trouble lay ahead for Grandpa if something happened to us. I was glad not to be in his shoes, and at the same time I knew I needed to behave so he didn't get into trouble because of us.

---

32 *The History of Wisconsin,* by John D. Buenker, Volume IV, pg. 221.

Although we lived less than a mile from their place, it was considered that we lived *in town*, so going to the farm and watching the animals being fed, was the best part of visiting them on the weekends, and I didn't want to lose that privilege. Every time we went out, Grandpa Charly grabbed his cane and we trailed behind him towards the barnyard.

Another Hulda commandment related to sitting in Grandpa Charly's chair. It was of sturdy wood construction and was called a "Captain's" chair. Its concave back and smooth armrests surrounded you when sitting in it. Grandpa's Captain chair served two purposes: One was for enjoyment, to sit in while eating or reading the paper at the dining room table. The second was for monitoring, when he finished eating, he would turn and slide his chair back from the table to the window directly behind him, and watch what was going on outside, including the barnyard activity. When not placed at the table, the chair stood guard next to the dining room window.

Grandma didn't have to scold us often because we were pretty well-behaved children, but occasionally we'd forget and she'd remind us in dry tone and without a hint of sympathy or a smile: *"That's Grandpa's chair. He'll want to sit there when he comes in the house. Go find another place to sit."*

Yes Ma'am!

Grandma had her personal chair too and it was understood that we definitely didn't sit there either. Hers was a Victorian-era chair with wooden arm rests and legs, an upholstered seat and backrest, always covered with a throw and pillows to support her. Her chair was next to the living room picture window[33] on the south side of the house. When sitting in her chair, Grandma could see the part of the yard where the children played, her vegetable and flower garden, and any passing traffic on Griswold Street, along with keeping an eye on the incoming weather (an important and common rural activity).

---

33 A "Picture" window is a large, usually single paned window, that provides a broad outside view. For many, sitting next to a picture window could provide hours of quiet entertainment.

Photo showing the picture window in the house where Grandma Hulda sat by, circa 1920. My father Clarence on the bicycle, and his four younger sisters, Meita, Grace, Verna & Laura seated. Kuehn Family Collection.

From her position in the living room, she could also see into the dining room, the passageway into the kitchen, with a partial view of the backdoor and the stairway leading to the second floor. In other words, she watched everyone's coming and going.

Looking out beyond the yard, was the street which provided most of the entertainment. An ideal place for watching the world go by while she knitted or mended while the sunrays filtered in. Located on the south side of the house it provided the most natural light making it also an ideal spot for Grandma to sit and read her bible, which she frequently

Winter view, circa 1930. Verna is building a snowman in the side yard. Notice the car on Griswold street (center photo) and the horses pulling a sled (right photo). Kuehn Family Collection.

did. On sunny days in the winter, it was the perfect place for taking a nap as it was one of the warmer places in the house.

When other adult family members were present, Grandma Hulda often conversed with them in German, especially if us kids were around. My aunts and uncles knew enough German that they understood her and could reply back. We were told they spoke German because they were discussing something that we as children needn't know and therefore couldn't repeat. At a young age I understood the point being made in the phrase adults often used: "Little pitchers have big ears." Not being able to understand German at times gave me the feeling of being left out.

During nice weather Grandpa would take us along to feed the animals or show us around the farmstead. Every season had its mystery and beauty. In summertime, playing hide and seek outdoors with one of our many aunts kept us active and laughing. In the winter, when we needed to stay indoors because of the weather, I loved playing the board game Old *Hogan's Goat* which kept us entertained for quite a while, sometimes until it was time go back home.

The game had a rhyme about a goat printed on the board itself. It made us giggle when we recited it every time we played,

> "Old Hogan's goat was feeling fine,
> he ate 3 red shirts off the line.
> I took a stick and broke his back
> and tied him to the railroad track.
> Old Hogan's goat though sick with pain,
> Coughed up the shirts and flagged the train."

During Christmas time, exposed in our grandparents' dining room was a large and beautifully crafted snow globe containing a winter scene. The globe was kept hidden in a hutch with glass doors where the good dinnerware and other family memorabilia was stored. I was always fascinated by how when the globe shook, it would create a magical-like snow fall inside. All the flakes of snow would go up, covering the house in a temporary winter storm, only to settle down, one by one by one. A metaphor for my grandparents' life. We were never allowed to touch or hold it but one of my aunts, Agnes or Laura, who still lived at home, would patiently shake it over and over again for us, and we never seemed to tire watching the idyllic Christmas scene become peaceful again.

Despite all the rules we had to follow at my grandparents' house, the memories of visiting them have always been pleasant ones.

Most women who worked on farms and took care of a household in the 1800s and 1900s, were extremely sensible, more out of necessity than personal desire. Neither of my parents, nor my grandparents, ever told us what it meant to be reared on a farm - it was just assumed we all knew, or that the type of work involved was "normal." It was only in doing research for this book, and reading the recollection below, that I was able to fully grasp how exhausting a day could be for a farm wife. Hamilton Holt collected stories in his volume "The Lives of Undistinguished Americans as Told by Themselves" and one in particular struck a chord with me. Although this is not Grandma Hulda's story, the farm work the writer describes is what is was like for grandma as well, during the years she spent on both the Metomen and Ripon home farms.

FARM WIFE – 1900
"I'm not a practical woman"[34]

"I have been a farmer's wife in one of the States of the Middle West for thirteen years, and everybody knows that the farmer's wife must of a necessity be a very practical woman, if she would be a successful one.

I am not a practical woman and consequently have been accounted a failure by practical friends and especially by my husband, who is wholly practical. . . . I was reared on a farm, was healthy and strong, was ambitious, and the work was not disagreeable, and having no children for the first six years of married life, the habit of going whenever asked to became firmly fixed, and he had no thought of hiring a man to help him, since I could do anything for which he needed help.

. . . I was an apt student at school and before I was eighteen I had earned a teacher's certificate of the second grade and would gladly have remained in school a few more years, but I had, unwittingly, agreed to marry the man who is now my husband, and though I begged to be released, his will was so much stronger that I was unable to free myself without wounding a loving heart, and could not find it in my nature to do so. This is a vague, general idea of how I spend my time; my work is so varied that it would be difficult, indeed, to describe a typical day's work.

Any bright morning in the latter part of May I am out of bed at four o'clock; next, after I have dressed and combed my hair, I start a fire in the kitchen stove, and while the stove is getting hot I go to my flower garden and gather a choice, half-blown rose and a spray of bride's wreath, and arrange them in my hair, and sweep the floors and then cook breakfast.

---

34 From "The Lives of Undistinguished Americans as Told by Themselves" by Hamilton Holt (1906). The name of the female author who wrote the narrative is not listed

While the other members of the family are eating breakfast I strain away the morning's milk (for my husband milks the cows while I get breakfast), and fill my husband's dinner pail, for he will go to work on our other farm for the day.

By this time it is half-past five o'clock, my husband is gone to his work, and the stock loudly pleading to be turned into the pastures. The younger cattle, a half-dozen steers, are left in the pasture at night, and I now drive the two cows, a half-quarter mile and turn them in with the others, come back, and then there's a horse in the barn that belongs in a field where there is no water, which I take to a spring quite a distance from the barn; bring it back and turn it into a field with the sheep, a dozen in number, which are housed at night.

The young calves are then turned out into the warm sunshine, and the stock hogs, which are kept in a pen, are clamoring for feed, and I carry a pail full of swill to them, and hasten to the house and turn out the chickens and put out feed and water for them, and it is, perhaps, 6.30 A.M.

I have not eaten breakfast yet, but that can wait; I make the beds next and straighten things up in the living room, for I dislike to have the early morning caller find my house topsy-turvy. When this is done I go to the kitchen, which also serves as a dining-room, and uncover the table, and take a mouthful of food occasionally as I pass to and fro at my work until my appetite is appeased.

By the time the work is done in the kitchen it is about 7.15 A. M., and the cool morning hours have flown, and no hoeing done in the garden yet, and the children's toilet has to be attended to and churning has to be done.

Finally the children are washed and churning done, and it is eight o'clock, and the sun getting hot, but no matter, weeds die quickly when cut down in the heat of the day, and I use the hoe to a good advantage until the dinner hour, which is 11.30 A. M. We come in, and I comb my hair, and put fresh flowers in it, and eat a cold dinner, put out feed and water for the chickens; set a hen, perhaps, sweep the floors again; sit down and rest, and read a few moments, and it is nearly one o'clock, and I sweep the door yard while I am waiting for the clock to strike the hour.

I make and sow a flower bed, dig around some shrubbery, and go back to the garden to hoe until time to do the chores at night, but ere long some hogs *come up to the back gate, through the wheat field, and when I go to see what is wrong I find that the cows have torn the fence down, and they, too, are in the wheat field.*

With much difficulty I get them back into their own domain and repair the fence. I hoe in the garden till four o'clock; then I go into the house and get supper, and prepare something for the dinner pail to-morrow; when supper is all ready it is set aside, and I pull a few hundred plants of tomato, sweet potato or cabbage for transplanting, set them in a cool, moist place where they will not wilt, and I then go after the horse, water him, and put him in the barn; call the sheep and house them, and go after the cows and milk them, feed the hogs, put down hay for three horses, and put oats and corn in their troughs, and set those plants and come in and fasten up the chickens, and it is dark. By this time it is 8 o'clock P. M.; my husband has come home, and we are eating supper; when we are through eating I make the beds ready, and the children and their father go to bed, and I wash the dishes and get things in shape to get breakfast quickly next morning.

It is now about 9 o'clock P. M., and after a short prayer I retire for the night."

At the back of my grandparent's house was a porch where certain chores were always done. In winter and summer the space was used for churning butter and for storage. Large pots and pans for canning fruits and vegetables were also kept there, as was their early century washing machine.

The washing machine arrived in Ripon in 1908 when Joe Barlow and John Seelig, who ran a hardware store in Ripon, "bought several hand-powered washing machines...." and began experimenting to improve them, later buying the rights to manufacture their own version. These first washing machines saved a lot of time and hard work by mechanically swirling and plunging the clothes inside a tub containing soap and water. Later versions of the machine included a side attachment called a "wringer," consisting of two rollers through which the garments were run to squeeze out excess water before hanging them out on the line to dry.

During the summer, the back porch was kept open on all sides. An overhead roof provided shade and an open-air area for food preparation work or canning (to avoid heating yourself up inside next to the kitchen stove.) In wintertime, though, Grandpa Charly would enclose the porch, including the back door, with panels he had constructed out of lumber. The enclosure protected the back entry from the prevailing northwest wind and the harsh blowing snow during the long Wisconsin winter months. It was also a sheltered space to brush the snow off, or remove one's overshoes and hang heavy coats to dry before entering the house.[35]

Visiting my grandparents was a comforting experience in winter. It was always deliciously warm but if one still felt chilly, you would be invited to stand on the furnace grate. Standing on the grate in your socks with the rising heat from the furnace (which was in the basement) was an overall heavenly feeling. If we happened to stop in for a visit on a weekend afternoon, there always was the rich onion/herb smell of something cooking. On a Saturday it might be a chicken roasting for the noon meal on Sunday (because of church services on Sunday, there wasn't time to prepare a meal, so it was prepared the day before). On a Sunday it might be the buttery smell of fresh popcorn as an afternoon snack (using kernels from the farm). With the house being closed-up during the cold weather and not allowed to air out, all those rich good kitchen scents lingered around. The most enjoyable of them being my grandmother's freshly baked sourdough bread. It was not a sourdough as we know it today, but it was bittersweet and the long-lasting aroma from the freshly baked bread filled every single inch of the house.

The freshly baked bread you remember eating as a child at home, or at your grandmother's, always holds a special place in one's heart,

---

35 Any family member or friends coming to visit would have known to come to the back of the house which was the main, daily entrance door. There was a front door but it was inside an enclosed porch. Many farm houses had front doors facing the street or road but they were not used for entry because the driveway typically ran alongside the house and led to the farm buildings in the back. As in most rural areas, there were no sidewalks either.

and no other bread will ever come close to it. I've often wondered how Grandma Hulda made her bread, if it was second nature, or if she actually followed a recipe. When my brother Carl sent me my mother's old cookbook, I thought I might find Grandma's bread recipe tucked inside, but I didn't. Instead I came across a technique I had completely forgotten and that could "make or break" one's breadmaking: The method for testing oven temperature to ensure its correctness for baking - a method I saw my Grandmother and my mother use consistently.

Like most families in the early 1900s, my grandparents had a wood burning iron stove in their kitchen. Most stoves didn't have a thermometer, so to test if the oven was hot enough the instruction given in the bread recipe was, "if a piece of paper placed in the oven turned dark brown within five minutes that means the oven is hot and at the right temperature for baking bread."[36] Cookstoves back then burned wood or coal to heat them, so there was only one way to regulate oven temperature and that was by propping the oven door open for a few minutes letting enough heat out to prevent what was being baked from burning.

Another one of those memorable "Grandma's House" afternoon aromas was that of fried potatoes, one of my Hulda favorites. The smell would waft its way out of the kitchen greeting you as you approached the house. During my grandparent's time, as well as my childhood, foods were usually fried in butter, lard, or bacon grease, which always added richness of flavor to any dish. But for the most part, I loved all of grandma's dishes. During my childhood what was prepared for meals is what you ate; if you didn't like what was being served you ate it anyway or you went hungry and had to wait until the next meal. There was no snacking back then, and it was rare that there were any leftovers. That was not an era for fussy eaters. I don't recall if Grandma's baking and cooking was better than anyone else's. If there was a family gathering where everyone brought dishes and desserts to share, you would always know you could depend on Grandma's or your own mother's dish. If you were

---

36 The Wisconsin News Cookbook, 1932 Edition. "Wheat Bread," pg. 15-16.

an adventurous eater and tried something someone else had brought, and liked it, all the better. I was always of the mindset that I knew what Grandma's and my mother's cooking tasted like, so out of sheer childhood curiosity I always tried something new.

The summertime always provided memorable experiences. It was at a young age that I learned to love Grandma's summer dill pickles. The pickles started out as small cucumbers picked from her garden, with dill being a staple in her vegetable patch. The cucumbers and dill, along with garlic for flavoring, were layered into a five-gallon earthen crock[37] into which a salt, water, and vinegar brine was poured, filling the container almost to the brim. Then it was placed outdoors to sit and marinade on the back porch. The crock had a wooden cover that was held in place with a heavy stone from the garden. The stone served two purposes: to block the cover tightly in place, and to keep out small, "unwanted plunderers." Grandma placed the crock where it would receive the most sun exposure during the day, setting in the fermentation process. In a week's time, the dill pickles were ready to be enjoyed.

I have a strong visual memory of the pickle experience. Grandma was dressed in her typical summertime attire, a shapeless, patterned cotton dress covered by an apron. She'd slide the wooden crock cover to one side, and stick her thick hand halfway down into the container to retrieve a pickle that she would slice into pieces for each of us saying, *"now here's a taste, you can have more at mealtime."* Nothing else felt that refreshing during the summer as the tangy crunch of one of her homemade dill pickles.

---

37 A "crock" is a cylindrical shaped earthenware vessel that originated in the Rhineland area of Germany in the 15th century. It became popular in 19th century North America and is also known as "stoneware". Crocks were used to store foods but also for fermentation processes and pickling. They helped families survive winters by storing and keeping their foods and came in different sizes and shapes, from 20 gallons to pint-sized jugs that used corks to keep in the flavor of its contents. They are still used significantly in the Midwest and some are even considered collector's items.

My Last Visit with Grandma

It was on a fall evening back in 1948, the time of year when the sun sets in the late afternoon causing temperatures to be chilly enough to warrant a jacket, that my father took our family to visit Grandma Hulda. Something seemed different about this trip. Typically, our family didn't go visiting on a weekday evening during the school year, and certainly not after dark unless it was a holiday visit, and this was not a holiday.

I knew Grandma had been ill for some time, and I wasn't so young as to not understand it was something serious, but as children we hadn't been told any details about what was troubling her. Over time, when we visited her, I noticed that she had become less and less active, and a more serious mood prevailed among the adults when we were there. I always wished she would get well and things would go back to being the way they were "before." We had become accustomed to her routines and knew what to expect. Now, because of her deteriorating health, the situation had an ominous feel in that something could happen that would take us into the unknown. I was twelve years old and had never experienced the feeling of impending loss of a loved one. And I was afraid. The difficulty of getting around forced her to sit in her chair most of the day. The only time I would see her leave the chair was to get a drink of water. She would slowly shuffle her way to the kitchen, her weathered slippers sanding the floor, to where the drinking water pail stood on the counter by the sink. Every country home had a water pail, theirs was of a white enamel inside and out, with a red rim. Some of the color was chipped on the rim and around the bottom. A long-handled aluminum dipper (like a ladle) hung on the side. This was the drinking water that had been carried into the house early that morning from the well pump out in the yard. Grandma would grasp the handle of the dipper filling it as she lifted it from the pail, then bring it to her mouth and taking a long refreshing drink directly from the dipper. Everyone drank from the same dipper, we were all family and shared everything as needed, without thinking about it twice.

By the time of our unexplained evening visit, she had not been attend-ing church for months, which meant something was definitely wrong, as she was a devout person and we all participated in the same church service every Sunday, at the Immanuel Evangelical United Brethren Church in Ripon.

She increasingly spent time in her sleeping room, a small side cham-ber just off from the living room. It didn't have a door, only a floor length drape hanging from a rod, usually pushed to one side, but that could be pulled across the opening if privacy was needed. It was small, perhaps a ten by ten-foot space, which also served as my grandparent's bedroom (although to us it was known as "the sleeping room"). Sparsely furnished, it had two single beds, one against each wall, with about two or three feet in between. Inside the room, against the wall at the foot of Grandma's bed on the left, was a makeshift closet where they hung their *good* clothes (visiting dresses or Sunday outfits).

It always seemed dark in that room, and the only decorations I remember being was their framed wedding picture on one wall and on the opposite, a framed religious picture of *Jesus Praying in The Garden of Gethsemane.* In keeping with the thought of that picture one of Grandma's favorite church songs was *In The Garden.* The first few words said, "I come to the garden alone..." and provided an insight to her devout Evangelical persona. Her religion was very important and personal to her, and her love for the outdoors too, especially with her garden being one of her prized places to connect with nature in a spiritual way.

As we entered the house that evening, my Dad said to us *"Grandma wants to see you kids. But not all four at the same time."* The four of us were usually paired, me with my sister Elaine, we two being a year apart in age, and then my oldest sister Alice with my younger brother Carl, who were five years apart in age.

I felt uncomfortable going into her private sleeping room with her lying in bed. I had never been in there when someone was resting. The room was dark, with the only light coming through the doorway from a lamp in the living room. There was a window in the center of the back wall, about as wide as the space between the two beds and a window that looked out onto the front porch. It could have been a luminous room but because it was already dark outside, the windows didn't provide any light. Grandma was lying in bed, with her head toward the back wall, where she could see into the living room when the door drape was open.

Elaine and I entered the room cautiously, not knowing why she had asked to see us since she had never done so before. As we approached the doorway, requesting permission to enter, Elaine explained that our father had told us to come see her.

Grandma Hulda opened her eyes and motioned for us to come in. She said she wasn't sleeping, just resting. She mentioned feeling bad for not having had much chance to see any of us children when we came to visit lately and gestured that we could sit on Grandpa's bed if we wanted to.

As we edged ourselves up onto Grandpa's mattress she began the conversation by asking how we were doing in school, and if we had been going to church and Sunday School regularly. She said church was important to her and she missed going since she had become ill.

Then she began to tell us a story, speaking slowly in English, as if measuring every word.

"When Grandpa and I married, I felt so grown up... But thinking back after many years I realized how young I was. I grew up in a large family - I quickly learned, everyone had chores to do. For we girls it was to help with housework, making meals and taking care of my younger brother Adolph and my younger sisters Otelia and Martha. Even though there was not much difference in age I had to help them get dressed, walk them two miles to school, and then help with their lessons from school too. The boys had to help with outdoor chores and farm work. I learned something too. Growing up being part of a family is much differ-ent than being responsible for a family. After I married your Grandpa I found I was in a family-way. We weren't even married a year and now I had a baby to care for. That's when I found out what being a parent and taking care of a child was about. In my family while growing up, and during my married life with my and Grandpa's family, everyone accepted responsibility. You can't always depend

on other family members or someone else to help you because they have their chores to do too. But, you always knew they were there if you needed them.

When your Uncle Frederick was born, I was happy but afraid at the same time. I had never been away from home until Grandpa and I left my parent's house and moved to Brandon. I was so happy to be married. Your Grandpa was a good man and I wanted to start my own life away from home. I was afraid of course. I didn't know if I could be a good wife. But I tried and worked hard and took care of your Grandfather, helping him as much as I could.

Then our family kept growing. After your Uncle Frederick was born, your Uncle Walter came, then your Aunt Agnes and your Uncle Benjamin while we lived on the Brandon farm. We had many children to care for and life wasn't easy for us, but Grandpa and I managed to make sure everyone was fed and clothed, and to do that your Grandpa worked so hard. Then, after a few years we decided to leave Brandon so your Grandpa could find other work to earn extra money. A year after we moved to our farm here in Ripon your father Clarence was born and then came your aunts Laura, Meita, Grace and Verna. We had a large family that we were responsible for. We had many mouths to feed, but we didn't feel poor, even if sometimes there was only enough to scrape by on. The first few years after moving to Ripon were difficult, one year was especially hard.

After saying this, she paused and took a deep difficult breath, adjusting the blanket covering her legs. My sister and I sat so very still, silent as rocks. We eagerly listened to what was going to be the first and last story Grandma would ever tell us though we didn't know it at the time. She took another deep breath, folded her hands together over her chest and continued.

One year Grandpa and I didn't know how we would make it. It was late winter or early spring and all we had left to eat in the cellar were potatoes. The canned goods were all used up and we didn't have money to buy anything else. One day I went down to the potato bin and realized it was almost empty; that year's crop hadn't been so good. Usually we had enough to tide us over until there were fresh vegetables from the garden in the spring. The potatoes that were left in the bin were withered, not good, dried out because they were so old.

I started gathering what I would need for that day's meal when I picked up what I thought was a potato but it felt different. It was dark in the cellar and I couldn't see in the storage bin so I just put it in the basket anyway. Then I went upstairs to wash and peel the potatoes. There was more light in the kitchen, so I looked for that strange potato it in the basket. I found it and realized it wasn't a potato but a money pouch with some coins inside. I was surprised, this had never happened to me before. I set it aside on the window sill above the counter and continued preparing supper. When Grandpa came back from work, I told him what I found and asked if he had put it in the potato bin. He said he hadn't and was surprised like I was. We agreed it didn't belong to anyone in our house.

We didn't know whose it was, or who to return it to. I felt it was a sign that our faith was helping us through this difficult time. We were thankful for those few coins, they made it possible to buy something else to eat for those remaining weeks."

After a brief silence, she looked us in the eyes and with a resigned smile added *"I just wanted you to know that whatever happens, I've had a good life."* Then she laid her head on the pillow as if she felt relieved and held out her hand to touch ours as we slid down off Grandpa's bed. We had sat there listening to Grandma's story without saying a word, and then as we knew it was time, I touched her warm hand and left the room.

A strong sadness washed over me, even if I did not completely understand what was happening. That story she told us changed the way I thought about Grandma Hulda forever. Suddenly there was so much more to her, and I appreciated her presence immensely.

During the short ride home that night no one said a word. When we walked into our house, my Dad uttered in a low voice *"It's bedtime, tomorrow is a school day."* That night I lay in bed thinking about everything she had said to us. What was going to happen to her now? How come she never told us that story before? If my Dad knew that story why hadn't he told us? I was at the beginning of my adolescence, an age where already a lot of turmoil overwhelms one's mind, and I was discovering all these new, mixed, unhappy feelings which were slowly finding their place inside of me. I didn't like it.

Things began to slowly make sense. I had a better understanding of how being a Grandma was more than just cooking for everyone or giving us orders. I'd come to realize later in life, in fact when I was probably the age my father was at that time, that a true matriarch takes responsibility for the whole family, helping the children grow up to be good citizens, good people, and good family members. Grandma's message was about continuously caring for all those close to you and those who you helped bring into this world.

Affections. In our family we didn't hug or kiss, ever, or even say goodbye. Hugging the children was not something my grandparents or the other adults in our family ever did. It was just understood Grandma cared about us nonetheless. That fall evening visit with Grandma was within the last weeks or days of her life. I don't recall seeing her alive after that.

A few days after their fifty-fourth wedding anniversary, Grandma Hulda's heart gave up and she died in her own home of coronary sclerosis. It was November 8, 1948 and she was seventy years old. One of my aunts stopped by our house earlier that evening, after visiting her, and told us she thought Grandma was feeling better, which gave me a hopeful feeling. A couple of hours later however, the telephone rang and we were told Grandma was gone, having suffered a heart attack.

The funeral was held a few days later at the Ripon church our family always attended. This was my first funeral. I noticed an open casket in front of the altar. Prior to the service beginning, we walked together as a family to see her one last time. She wore the only dress I had ever seen her wear when not at home, a long black gown she always used for church. Her hands were clasped over her chest, holding her bible and her white handkerchief. My father asked us to say goodbye by touching her hand, which each of us reluctantly did when it was our turn.

Certain memories never leave us. I remember with utmost clarity her hand was cold, hard, unfamiliar. Nothing like the soft, warm, wrinkly hand I had touched just a few days earlier. The grandma I'd known and come to understand a little better, had left us. And just like that, amid strong and confusing emotions of love, sadness, denial, and bitter acceptance, she was buried at Woodlawn cemetery, in Ripon, that same day.

There was so much I still didn't know about her life, and so much I didn't question until I set out to write this book. Eventually the feelings of loss passed, but going to the farm was no longer the same. *What should we do? How were we supposed to act towards Grandpa Charly?* With Thanksgiving and Christmas approaching, how would we celebrate it if she wasn't here? My Dad took it very hard, he being the youngest son, especially close to his mother. I had never known this side of him either and I didn't like seeing him sad and not knowing what to do to make him feel better. But most of all, I didn't like Grandma not being there with us.

My grandparents had lived by the words from their wedding vows, each holding up their part of the promise "to love and to cherish, till death do us part."

Grandma Hulda was gone and now Grandpa Charly had been left alone.

CHAPTER 9

Grandpa Charly Kuehn, Part I

Grandpa Charly in his garden. Kuehn Family Collection.

The Essentials

IF GRANDMA HULDA WAS THE family matriarch, Grandpa Charly was the entrepreneur in the family. He was approaching seventy by the time I reached an age where I could start recalling events and people in my life and making sense of them. My childhood memories of him are of a likeable old man. People who had worked with him would always tell my father -after he took over the business- what a good fellow he was, a kind person, a quiet and true gentleman, who attended church regularly, had a subtle sense of humor and who never swore or used a curse word, ever. I never saw him smoke or use tobacco either, but he did have one little vice, and that was chewing gum... That was Grandpa Charly's thing. According to the book "Everyday Life in the 1800s" in that century and later, people who didn't chew tobacco often chewed *spruce gum*[38]. I don't know if he kept the sticks or pieces in his pocket, or hidden somewhere, as he never offered any of it to us kids and I never saw it in his house. As children we weren't allowed to have gum (especially in school). Besides, there were 4 of us children in my family and gum cost money, which was always an issue. On the rare occasion one of us would ask for something my father would say, "if I buy that for you I have to buy the same for each of you kids and we can't afford it."

Grandpa Charly's parents, William and Wilhelmine, married soon after immigrating to the United States in 1869. Charly was born a year later, on Sunday October 30th, 1870.

As the first child, and a male, certain privileges and responsibilities of birth order were his to take on. In addition, he was a first-generation immigrant, so there were values and standards that his parents upheld which he carried into his new family as well.

---

38 The Indians of New England taught American colonists to quench their thirsts by chewing the gum-like resin that forms on spruce trees when its bark is cut. In the early 1800s, lumps of this spruce gum were sold in the eastern United States, making it America's first commercial chewing gum. From www.wrigley.com, The History of Gum.

In my research regarding challenges immigrants faced when coming to the US, I came across a report from 2011 prepared by the APA Presidential Task Force on Immigration. Although this document was written a century after my great grandparents had come to the US, I feel it's findings resemble how the generations of my family also evolved over the decades. The report states that immigrants not only are resilient and resourceful but, like all human beings, they are influenced by their social context. "First-generation immigrant populations demonstrate the best performance on a variety of physical health, behavioral health, and some educational outcomes, followed by a decline in subsequent generations. Although many recently arrived immigrants face a wide range of stressors and risks (e.g., poverty, discrimination, taxing occupations, fewer years of schooling and social isolation), they do better than their counterparts who remain in the country of origin, as well as second-generation immigrants, on a wide range of outcomes."[39]

Grandpa Charly moved his new family to Metomen in 1895 because he knew he could provide a better life for them by working at his father's farm and, second, because his father surely needed his help in this new endeavor, making it the right thing to do as the first-born child. The demanding physical work was something my grandpa was already familiar with; at 25 years old, he had his whole life ahead of him to raise a family and become financially independent. Twelve years after going to Metomen, he would pick up and move with his family again, this time to the larger city of Ripon - just 7 miles away.

Historical documents like the Country-Life Reform by William Bowers[40], show that between 1900 through 1920 there was an accelerating trend of people moving away from the land and towards the cities, producing a noticeable decline of the farm population. For

39 American Psychology Association, "Crossroads: The Psychology of Immigration in the New Century" by Carola Suárez-Orozco, PhD, Chair, Dina Birman, PhD, J. Manuel Casas, PhD, Nadine Nakamura, PhD, Pratyusha Tummala-Narra, PhD, Michael Zárate, PhD.

40 Country-Life Reform, 1900-1920: A Neglected Aspect of Progressive Era History, published in Agricultural History, Vol. 45, No 3, (Jul,1971) pp.211-221, by the Agricultural History Society.

many, country life was beginning to lose its allure. A rural reform movement began to emerge, showing how farm profits had become inadequate, complaining that rural education was not up to par with was what happening in the world and that "love for country life" and "scientific farming methods" should be taught in schools. There was also discontent with the rural church, believing it wasn't promoting satisfaction with farm life and should teach and practice a social morality as urban churches did. "By 1900 over one-third of the farms in the nation were operated by tenants and although it was still possible to rise from hired hand to tenant to owner, the stepping stones were moving increasingly farther apart. To remedy this, some reformers advocated government aid to young men who wished to acquire farms."[41]

Records show that in 1907, twelve years after moving from Princeton to Metomen, Grandpa Charly was still listed as "farmer" but also had a second occupation as a "street sprinkler" (per the 1910 census), most likely to supplement his income. A couple of years later, whether because of need or personal desire, Grandpa is listed as "Truck Farmer" on Aunt Meita's birth certificate of 1913. By doing the fieldwork of growing the produce he had built a strong network of connections and moved away from farming to focus on distributing produce and other goods to area merchants. With time, this occupation eventually evolved into Grandpa's *drayage* work. His younger brothers were now at an age where they could take on larger responsibilities at his father's farm if he stepped away, and under William Sr.'s tutelage, they would strive to keep the family legacy and its economic stability going.

The dray work not only provided economic means for Grandpa to support his growing family, but would enable his own children to have steady work when the time came for them to contribute to the household. The business was established in 1919 and was called *C. A. Kuehn*

---

41 William L. Bowers, "Farmers and Reformers in an Urban Age: The Country life Movement and the 'Rural Problem,' 1900-1920," (Ph.D. dissertation, University of Iowa, 1968), chapter 5.

and son Drayage. He started the venture using a team of dray horses and wagons from his own farms until he could buy a truck - which were available by then in some of the larger cities. I came to learn that throughout the years Grandpa Charly had the dray business, he provided employment for all his sons and gave each of them the opportunity to take over the business and continue that line of work if they so wished.

When my father (Clarence), then Grandpa's youngest son, graduated from Ripon High School in 1927, he took over most of the dray work, allowing Grandpa Charly to finally take a step back from the daily operations. His involvement in farming and the drayage business had changed a lot by the time I was a youngster visiting his house. At 70, he was no longer working full time but helped if needed. My father continued managing the company for almost 10 years after Grandpa retired and was able to expand it to two dray trucks. I have a vague recollection as a young boy, probably about 4 years old, of my father leaving the house carrying a small valise. In questioning my mother as to where Daddy was going, and how long he would be gone, she told me he was off to South Bend, Indiana, to the Studebaker assembly plant to pick up his new truck and drive it home. I realize now this must have been an important event, it meant business was good and expanding, but she said it very matter-of-factly, without a hint excitement or enthusiasm in her voice, perhaps a reflection of how she felt about her own life or marriage in those days.

The "new" truck was between a 1939 and 1941 model. Vehicles were getting difficult to buy during those years with car and truck manufacturers changing over to production of military vehicles for World War II. My father had been told by the Studebaker dealer in Ripon, Bloedel and Suckow, that if he really wanted a new truck he would need to buy one directly at the factory while they were still available.

Our home on Ransom Street only had garage space for one truck, so the newer one was kept at home, and the older one, a 1936 Studebaker was kept in a shed at Grandpa Charly's farm, less than a mile away. We kids called the new one - also a Studebaker - the "Stub-nosed" truck.

Left, 1936 Studebaker, known to us as the "Old Truck".
Right, the "Stub-nose" 1940 Studebaker.

The new truck was used to haul goods, belongings and freight that needed to be kept "as clean as possible," such as household furniture, textiles or ingredients used at the local cookie factory.[42] The "Old Truck" was used instead for freight that was grimy, weathered, or cargo that arrived at the Ripon train station, covered in dust and soot from being shipped on open railroad cars. It also hauled the ashes and products of combustion of coal from the local schools and businesses which used coal burning stoker fired boilers.

RETIREMENT LIFE ON THE RIPON FARM

During his later years, after retiring, Grandpa Charly still kept a few animals at his farm. It was more "hobby farming," where anything that was produced was intended for family use. He had one cow for milk and dairy products, a few swine for pork and bacon, chickens for meat and eggs and a horse, Old Jim, for transportation around the area.[43]

In summer, his farm attire was always a long-sleeved chambray shirt buttoned at the wrists and neck (to protect him from insects, sun and

---

42 Ripon Foods Inc. was founded in 1930 with 25 employees. The privately held company produced cookies with its brand name of "Rippin Good." The original factory was on Fenton Street.

43 Ripon Historical Society, 1946 Ripon City Tax Records show he was assessed property taxes on "two head of livestock, one swine and thirty chickens." The livestock were his horse "Jim" and a cow or heifer.

Another of Ripon's oldtimers is Charles Kuehn, former drayman and local truck farmer, who celebrated his 80th birthday here recently. Mr. Kuehn has nine children, Clarence, Walter, Laura, Agnes and Ben of Ripon; Fred of Fond du Lac; Mrs. Meta Page, Green Lake; Mrs. Verna Taves, Lamartine, and Mrs. Grace Rispelja, Alto. There are 17 grandchildren and 7 great-grandchildren.

The Ripon Commonwealth weekly newspaper ran a series on local business persons upon reaching their 80th birthday. Charly was mentioned in 1950. Courtesy Ripon Commonwealth Press.

any scrapes or scratches), denim bib overalls or the waist-high type with suspenders, and his worn brown Fedora hat. If we happened to be visiting when it was time for him to do his farm chores, he would grab his trusty old cane and take me and my siblings to the barnyard to feed the animals. He knew how much we enjoyed seeing them and at the same time, without us realizing it, he was teaching us a thing or two about the basics of farm life.

During the warmer months, the sweet smell of newly harvested hay filled the barnyard air. When I come across that scent these days, while driving through the countryside in rural Wisconsin, I'm immediately drawn back to the memory of standing next to Grandpa Charly in his barn. The lower level of the horse barn housed the stalls where he kept Jim, and a separate room which he used as a workshop. Tools were strewn all over the workbench, often making me wonder how he could find anything. In that same room was the anvil and instruments for maintaining and shoeing Jim's hoofs.

The loft of the horse barn stored all the hay. We were only allowed to look up into it while Grandpa Charly held the door open for us, but never, under any circumstances were we allowed to crawl up in there. Grandpa feared we could fall down the chute (used to push hay into the manger), something that to me always sounded like it would be great fun. However, we never questioned the reason or thought about the possible danger, we just did as we were told. An adults' reprimand weighed more to us than possibly getting injured, or not being allowed to go out with Grandpa Charly again.

One thing that fascinated us was how Grandpa got water from the well in front of the house over to the barnyard for the livestock to drink. In the ground, underneath the spigot of the well pump, was a metal cover with holes drilled in it. When Grandpa pumped water, it would come out the spigot, fall and disappear through the drilled holes. Knowing this was a source of entertainment for the kids, he would tell us to run across the driveway, look over the ledge of the wall, and watch for the water to magically run out of the wall and into a large cast iron container from which the animals could drink. It didn't register with us at that young, naive age, that there was an underground pipe the water traveled through, saving the need to fill pails throughout the day and carry them to the tank. And being Grandpa Charly, he never told us this either. We all beamed with awe and disbelief as the water arrived from one place to the other.

Water for the chickens however still needed to be carried in a pail from the well pump to the chicken coop to fill their own drinking fountains. Water needed for pig slop, sometimes called "swill"[44], was gathered from the water tank and then poured into pails where it was mixed with the other food scraps. From there he carried it over to the pig pen and poured the slop into their feeding trough. In the end, a single water pump provided entertainment for us children, as well as gave life to so many animals and plants on the farm, which in turn fed us for so many years. So many simple things brought us joy back then, and still today, even if in memory.

Occasionally, during warmer weather we were allowed to wander around his farm on our own. One of the favorite places my younger brother and I would go to was behind the horse barn to snoop around the machine shed. It gave us "unsupervised time" outdoors, away from where the adults were visiting and talking about stuff we were never interested in. Poking around in the shed provided an opportunity for adventure and to exercise our imagination about what each item was probably used for. It was a chance for us to pretend we were Grandpa Charly.

Inside the shed were old horse-drawn farm implements, a hay mower and rake, a walk-behind plow, and a single horse carriage with a canopy top. There was also a "cutter"[45] that could be hitched to Jim, the type one pictures in the song Jingle Bells when it refers to "a one horse open sleigh."

---

44 Swill was a mixture of water, ground shelled corn and food scraps, either from meal preparation or leftovers, that was fed daily to the pigs.

45 A "cutter" is a light sleigh used for transportation of people, specifically in winter when there is snow. Smaller than a sleigh, it usually fits two people quite snug. A sleigh is larger and accommodates more people. The runners on cutters are further apart than in sleighs, because cutters were made for long and slow travel, allowing the cutter to go straight most of the time, but making it harder to maneuver, requiring it to make careful, wider turns.

One item we liked to play with was a one-cylinder gas engine. It had a flywheel on each side that when we turned it, made a sound as if it were going to start and run. We were always disappointed when it didn't get going - and although we knew it never had, we'd always try it in the hopes one day it magically would (at an older age I discovered the sound we were so excited about was only compressed air escaping when a valve opened.)

These were things Grandpa Charly had accumulated over the years when he had been farming and during the time he had his dray business. He probably felt the items still had some value, or that some of the scrap iron could be recycled and repurposed. Another possibility is that having been a man that came from so little, like so many others of his generation, he might have not been able to bring himself to part with these things, thinking he'd find a use for them "someday."

During freezing weather Grandpa didn't take us along to feed the animals because it was too cold for us to be outside. He just wanted to get the chores done as quickly as possible and to come back indoors. Winter was a whole other ballgame in this part of Wisconsin. Schedules, routines, and clothing changed to adapt to the extreme temperature shifts that took place. When it was chore time, I used to see him get up out of his captain's chair by the window, and go sit on the one by the kitchen's back door to get ready. He'd pull on knee-high rubber boots over his wool boot liners; liners which he wore on his feet and sometimes walked around the house in. Under the liners, were his warm wool socks.

His farm attire didn't change much in the winter. Just as in the summer, over his undershirt he wore a long-sleeved flannel shirt buttoned up to the neck and at the wrists. He used the same overalls but with Long John's underneath to keep the cold air from seeping in. He'd then go out to the back porch, which was boarded up this time of the year, and finish dressing himself by putting on his plaid wool jacket, wool cap with fur lined ear flaps, and leather mittens which had a sturdy wool knit inner lining.

Countrymen brought their sleighs loaded with firewood for sale to
the Square in downtown Ripon. Courtesy Ripon Main Street, Inc.

In Wisconsin winter often starts in late October, and can last all
the way through April, with harsh low temperatures commonly reaching below zero throughout January and February. In fact, "During more
than one-half of the winters, temperatures fall to -40 F or lower, and
almost every winter temperatures of -30 F or colder are reported from
northern stations."[46] The only way to do the farm work outdoors was to
heavily layer up, but even in doing so, the cold could always be felt. The
layers just mitigated the feeling of how winter could be cruel on the body.

---

46 Source: University of Wisconsin Extension, Wisconsin State Climatology Office,
Climate of Wisconsin.

Certain rituals Grandpa had have stayed with me after all these years. Rituals that I looked upon with awe as a child, I now remember with great fondness as an adult. Grandpa Charly always prepared for washing up or shaving at the kitchen sink. He'd be in his undershirt, with his outer shirt stripped to the waist, suspenders still buttoned to his pants but hanging down each side. The razor he used for shaving fascinated me. It had two curved parts that fit together like spoons (designed to hold the double-edged blade). But, there was another gadget that was even more interesting, and that was his TwinPlex Razor Blade Stropper, a device used to sharpen and reuse the blades rather than throwing them away. When the blade was placed into the sharpening tool, a handle rotated the drums, covered in strop leather, that would hone the edge of the blade to sharpen it.[47] I can still remember the noise it made as the crank flicked the leather against the blade over and over, sharpening it without grinding it, so the edges would be well honed, providing a close shave."

TwinPlex razor blade stropper.

---

47 Twinplex was a company based out of Chicago. Their first stropper was invented in 1910.

There is another memory I've held onto dearly, about another one of his daily routines. Around the early 1950s, in the evening, Charly enjoyed catching up on the day's news while sitting at the dining room table reading the Milwaukee Journal the paperboy delivered to the house. His aging hands had enlarged knuckles, the kind only years of intense farming and hard labor could bring. His bent finger joints grasped the pages of that light weight newspaper with an unintentional strength. As a child, those hands seemed so strong and large to me. If they could talk, their story would also tell how gentle they could be when holding the tiny hand of one of his grandchildren as they learned to walk. They'd speak of the long days of repetitive physical work when it was time for planting or harvesting; of carrying equipment and moving heavy animals out to pasture, or down the fields for plowing. The same two hands that years later moved freight and goods for local people and businesses. Hands which provided for his family, and the generations of Kuehns to come after him.... For my father and his siblings, and for my siblings and me.

After reading the newspaper and before it was time for him to go to bed, Grandpa took his "daily medicine." As children, we didn't often visit late into the evening so it was with great interest that when we were there, we witnessed this "Charly moment." The medicine was brought out by my Aunt Agnes from some hidden place in a kitchen cabinet, and set in front of him at the dining room table. It was an amber colored liquid served in a tiny glass, hardly even a swallow, along with a glass of water. I recall questioning what was in that glass Grandpa was given, having never been given that type of medicine when I was sick. Sensing our curiosity, Aunt Agnes always said, "it's for Grandpa's heart and to help him sleep."[48] After Grandpa swallowed his medicine he would hook his

---

48 Alcohol was known as an ancient therapy that still held medicinal value with some older physicians. It could be prescribed for a variety of ailments including anemia, high blood pressure and heart disease to name a few, which were conditions Grandpa Charly had been diagnosed with by that time in his life. *Medicinal alcohol and Prohibition,* Melnickmedicalmuseum.com/2010/04/07/medicinal-alcohol-and-prohibition.

lower lip over his mustache, his "cookie duster" as he called it, to wring out any spillover drops. He then washed it all down with water and set it back on the table, closing the "medicine moment" with a long sigh of satisfaction.

My cousin Shirley shared with me another family tale from about the same time. After Hulda passed away, she sometimes stayed the night at Grandpa's place, when her parents had gone out. Before going to bed, Aunt Agnes would prepare and serve them "milktoast" a delicious childhood treat. Our aunt would take some toasted bread, break it into small pieces, put it into a bowl with warm milk, and pour a bit of sugar or maple syrup over it.[49] Little Shirley and Grandpa Charly would relish this as their "bedtime snack." Considering that the evening meal (supper) had been served at five o'clock, I can't imagine a better way to end the day before going to bed than with homemade milktoast.

GRANDPA CHARLY, THE MAN OUTSIDE THE FARM.

I don't ever recall seeing Grandpa drive anything other than his wagon with his horse Jim, harnessed and hitched to it. The wagon was of the same type seen in western movies. Tall skinny wheels, no canvas top, low sideboards, and a wooden plank for a seat. There was room behind the seat in the box of the wagon for hauling light loads like empty produce crates, scrap lumber or old shed tools. Another name for that type of buggy was a "runabout."

That rig was his means of transportation wherever he went. Sometimes he would pick up withered produce, no longer fresh and able to be sold,

---

49 Milk Toast was a popular food, usually eaten at breakfast, during the late 19th and 20th century, given to children or the convalescent because it was considered caloric and easy to digest. My mother's recipe from *The Wisconsin News Cookbook* stated: Melt two tablespoons of butter, add one tablespoon flour and brown. Stir in two cups of milk and one-half teaspoon salt. Stir and heat until this thickens slightly. Pour over slices of dry toast. Serve hot, *The Wisconsin News Cookbook, 1932 Edition, p. 27.*

from behind the grocery stores and bring it home to feed to the chickens or the pigs.

He also collected wooden produce crates, much needed, that he could break apart and use as kindling wood for starting the furnace fire downstairs or in the kitchen cookstove. One of my grandfather's regular routes from the farm to downtown Ripon was to head with Old Jim east on Griswold Street then turn left on Woodside Avenue, passing on the way Roosevelt Elementary School. My siblings and I, being all close in age, attended that school at the same time for a few years.

During the mid-1940s, after the United States entered World War II and the automobile manufacturers changed over to producing vehicles for the military, new civilian cars and trucks were not readily available, so those who owned them would keep repairing the ones they had. Even during these years it would have been somewhat unusual to use a horse and wagon to go into town, but, that was Grandpa's only mode of transportation, other than to walk, and he had to share the streets with other vehicles, cars, trucks, and bicycles. It was during those years that my sister Elaine remembers sometimes she'd spot Grandpa Charly passing the school during recess, or when the children were outside. He'd always be wearing his old brown felt hat and sporting a pleased grin on his face. The kids would rush towards the sidewalk to wave at him and see Old Jim. My sister would proudly announce to her classmates "That's my Grandpa!"

In or about 1946, the time came when for reasons I never knew specifically, he had to give up driving his horse; I assumed the way one gives up the car keys when reflexes decline and it's no longer safe to be an elderly driver on the road. But, it seems the reason was that Old Jim's time had come up. My sister Elaine told me that one day we visited Grandpa Charly at the farm on another sad occasion. Elaine says that Old Jim was lying dead in the barnyard and that Aunt Agnes continuously scolded us whenever we would peek out the window, looking for the horse we had come to like so much, as if he were our own. Old Jim may have died, or was euthanized if it had been ill, but everyone was there at Grandpa's side waiting for the rendering plant truck (negatively referred to as the glue factory) to pick up the carcass. His horse and wagon were Grandpa's livelihood, his personal means of transportation, which provided him with a good measure of independence, so it was quite an adjustment to lose that freedom and the horse he had come to depend on. Now Grandpa Charly needed to depend on someone to take him to church, to visit friends or attend a family gathering. Simple, everyday tasks like going to the bank, seeing a doctor, or picking up feed for the few animals he kept, meant relying on someone else. The emotional and physical cost of no longer being able to drive himself around most likely affected his ability to feel useful to himself and the farm he had so patiently built over the years for his family. Seeing Old Jim go after so many years together must have also taken a toll on Grandpa.

Through farming and his dray business, as well as through church, Grandpa Charly had met a lot of people. Though he was by no means an extrovert, he did have a subtle social life. There are few critical stories about Charly in the family lore, but a one had some humor at his expense. Two versions of this story have survived over the years which tell about Charly enjoying life while he was in still in the dray business in Ripon.

The first version, edited for children's ears, was told to me by my older cousin Marceline. Apparently, among Charly's business acquaintances was a local merchant who ran a bakery with one of its specialties being fresh glazed doughnuts. Occasionally, during his trips into downtown Ripon, Charly would stop in to visit and stay a while chatting away and consuming so many of these doughnuts that by time he got home, he was feeling sick. This led to him not being hungry for supper causing Grandma Hulda to be angry and question what he had been up to.

The second version, and perhaps the truer one, was passed down from my aunt Grace, one of Charly's daughters, to her children and then relayed to me by my cousin Phillip. The story was that *occasion-ally* Hulda's unmarried youngest brother Adolf, who also lived in Ripon working as a stonemason, and Charly, would get together at one of the local taverns to have a pint, or two, and kibitz with the other men who were playing cards or billiards. The next day Grandpa Charly would stay home "sick," spending a day of shame in the barn, while Hulda would be in her room crying.

Those were different times back then, and what was considered trouble then, would probably pass as normal behavior today. Even at that, the story in today's context doesn't seem to be that drastic of an incident. After all, Charly was of German heritage and drinking beer now and then wasn't unusual. However, those times and the dynamics within this Evangelically devout family must have made this dreadful for Hulda. She was the family matriarch, which included laying down rules of conduct for the family, including Charly, based on her religious upbringing. By drinking, and by drinking probably too much, Charly had not only sinned in the eyes of the Evangelical Church, but had shamed the family, and especially Hulda. She may have felt it put her in a bad light in the sight of the community because Charly could have been seen by other business acquaintances in downtown Ripon and surely word of his conduct would find its way to members of their church. What's more, he had probably violated Prohibition laws - in effect from 1920 to 1933 - making drinking alcohol illegal. To add more fuel to the fire, Charly had been out with Hulda's own brother who had been raised in the same strict religious environment and, in her view, both should have known better, especially since Charly was being a bad example to her younger brother.

CHAPTER 10

Their Farmstead Story

My sketch of the new house and farmstead as seen
from the corner of Griswold Street.

LIFE'S MILESTONES 1895 - 1945

DURING THE TWELVE YEARS CHARLES lived and worked on his father's farm
(1895 through 1907), in addition to their son Fredrick, he fathered three
more children, at two year intervals, Walter (1897), Agnes (1900) and
Benjamin (1902).

By 1907, with his ever-growing family, and having established himself as a seasoned farmworker, Grandpa Charly picked up his belongings
and moved everyone from their rental property to a small farmstead he
purchased in the nearby city of Ripon, for $1,300. He probably contin-
ued to work with his father for some transitional time, but he had also

started to expand on his own by entering a truck farming operation. A "truck farmer" grows and hauls vegetables to stores to be resold in the retail market. Charly may have been growing vegetables (well paying cash crops) on his father's farm at the beginning of his branching out of the family business. This line of work would provide support and benefit his father's business, and his own family.

The land my Grandparents purchased in Ripon, at the corner of Griswold and Thomas streets is the only home I would come to know as theirs and where every single memory I have of them was created. The Ripon farmstead was not a vacant and empty lot, but already had a series of functional buildings making life on the farm as efficient as possible.

The existing land structures included a two-bedroom house, and a medium sized barn for 2 or 3 cows (Jerseys or Guernsey's, whose milk was rich with high butterfat). There was also a barn for the horses and goats, an indoor and outdoor pen for the swine, a working farm tool shed, the free-standing outdoor chicken coop, and an indispensable structure called "the outhouse." An outhouse is a small structure, separate from a main building, built over a pit latrine or a dry toilet. Commonly humble and utilitarian, they were made of lumber so they could easily be moved when the earthen pit filled up. My grandparents' house had a "two-holer," meaning it could accommodate two users at the same time if there was an urgency and others had the inclination to do so.

Outhouse pits depths varied depending on usage. Shallower pits allowed for quicker decomposition, and less seepage into the neighboring soil. However, large families sometimes chose to extend the single pit to form a long-covered trench, or connected series of covered pits, so that waste could be spread out over a larger surface area. Toilet paper was also not readily available everywhere, and many times old newspapers or catalogue pages were used in its place.

This move, not more than six miles away from where they had lived in Metomen, would prove to be the beginning of financial independence. A year after living in their new home, and after six years of no new children in the family, in May of 1908 Charles and Hulda welcomed another son, Clarence, my father.

Drawing from memory of my grandparent's farmstead.

With Charles continuing to work at his father's farm, plus earning what he could with his own farm, in the fall of 1909 they were able to satisfy the terms of the land contract, enabling them to take out a mortgage on the property, they had purchased the land in Ripon just two years before.

1910 opened a new decade, requiring another national census to be taken. Leafing through records, I was unable to find Charles Kuehn with that spelling of his name. A more in-depth search revealed the census enumerator had written his first name as "Charly." This is the first time his name was spelled more informally, particularly on a census document. Grandpa continued to use Charles, or the abbreviated form "Chas," on legal documents - even though his baptized name was Carl. I like to think he changed his name because by now, at forty years old, he had established himself in Ripon as his own person, rather than as William Sr.'s son, and adopted the name "Charly" as he would be known henceforward.

The many jobs and different responsibilities Grandpa Charly and grandma Hulda took on told me they had had a busy and full life, sacrificing for the future of their family. Later that same year, Hulda gave birth to a second daughter, whom they named Laura. By 1910 their oldest child Fred (15) had gone as far in school as was required, had taken a job outside the home and helped around the farm when needed. Walter (13), Agnes (10) and Benjamin (8), attended Brown school, did house chores, tended to the family's vegetable garden, and helped in keeping an eye on Clarence (2) and baby Laura.

Outgrowing the House

By 1911, with a family of eight, they had outgrown their living space. Since work was steady, the mortgage was getting paid and things were "in order," my grandparents expanded their house into more comfortable living quarters for all.

The most practical way to go about expanding was to build the new house around the old house, allowing the family to continue to live in certain portions of it during construction.

The new, two story house measured thirty feet on each of the four sides and provided nine hundred square feet of living space on each level. A full-length open front porch faced east, where the front door was located. This allowed the house to receive ample sunlight during the day and provided a place to sit and relax as well. I recall Aunt Agnes saying that when Fred, Walter, Ben, and Clarence were older, they used the porch as their sleeping space on hot summer nights and, that at holiday time, it was also used as cold storage for the baked goods, fruit cakes and cookies.

The interior of the house only had a few rooms, but could accommodate the large family. On the ground level were the dining and living rooms with a large opening connecting the two areas. In the floor, between those two rooms, was the furnace grate so heat could circulate equally into both.

Off the living room was a small space my grandparents used as their bedroom. It didn't have a door, just a curtain they would slide over to block any light or for privacy. On that same side was the wood stairway that lead to the second level, built directly over the basement stairway, as was typical, to save space. The kitchen was in the remaining area on the ground level; it included a sink, with adjacent counter space for the water bucket, the cookstove, some cabinets and a chair by the back door with coat hooks above it. It's important to note that, in the days before refrigerators, an ice box was used to keep perishable food from spoiling. For lack of kitchen space their ice box was located downstairs, in the cellar, which was accessible from the kitchen and the outdoors.

The second level, was divided in half with two large rooms, one for the boys and one for the girls. The rooms did not have doors and there wasn't a bed for every child, but as was custom then, children shared beds until the older children moved out and there was space to occupy their own beds without having to share. As the boys grew older they slept on the front porch, which had been enclosed. This new "room" allowed them to sleep there also in the winter, leaving the entire upstairs for the five girls.

Among these official documents given to me by my sister Alice were the receipts for everything involved in the house expansion: building materials from the George Middleton Lumber Company, located on Blackburn Street at the north end of Ripon (it later became Fullerton Lumber Company and currently is the Jaystone Terrace Apartments.) Roofing, paint, and miscellaneous hardware receipts were from the Ripon Hardware Company, located at 109 Watson Street, on the east side of the square. Other materials and hired labor came from the Fairwater branch of Stellmacher Brothers.

The hired labor, which included four men, worked a total of fifty-five "man" days at a rate of $3.00 per day. The complete cost for building the house, materials, and labor, as shown on the receipts, totaled approximately $700 and took about three months to build. All the building materials were obtained on open credit. It's unknown where Grandpa Charly got the house plans but it was a common floor plan as

Front and back of receipt from Stellmacher Bros for labor costs
to build the new house. Marked "paid," by Frank Stellmacher
on the back of the receipt. Kuehn Family Collection.

I discovered in driving around the local countryside. There are a great
many houses with a similar configuration.[50]

There was no indoor bathroom included in the new house plans
because at that time, no public sewer or water service was available at
that address. According to a City of Ripon Department of Public Works
plat map showing underground utilities, it wasn't until 1950 that city
water was extended out on Griswold street and onto the Kuehn farm
property, forty-three years after purchasing the farmstead.

---

50 While doing research for this book I found that a house plan, along with the
building material needed for that plan, could be bought from a Sears, Roebuck, and
Company catalog. However, the manpower to construct the house using the materials
provided were still the owner's responsibility. Based on the prices shown in the catalogue it proved more economical to build using local suppliers and labor.

There were methods of providing indoor bathroom facilities in those days, but that meant additional costs of plumbing fixtures. One commonly used practice, that my grandparents did not do, was to place a water holding tank in the upper level of the house, typically the attic, and gravity would then provide sufficient water pressure to flush a toilet and to provide water to other spigots in the house. This required pumping water up to the tank and a more elaborate septic system for the waste. In the end, it was less of an effort, and cheaper, just to carry water in from the well. For washing and bathing, water from the cistern in the basement was pumped into a container, then heated on the kitchen stove. The wastewater was commonly poured into the sink and allowed to drain into an underground septic well or, in the summer it was carried directly outdoors and used to water the garden. With no indoor plumbing and no toilet in the house, a hole was dug in the backyard, at a reasonable distance from the house, and an outhouse constructed and placed over it.

The new house was completed in the fall of 1911. To settle with the suppliers of material, hardware and labor Grandpa Charly renegotiated a new mortgage for one thousand dollars which would cover the remaining amount due on the property and building expenses. He had established himself as a trustworthy businessman and an excellent credit risk. He could borrow a significant amount of money on, essentially, a signature note.

1912 would pass with my grandparents and their family living more comfortably in their new house. In February of 1913, the family gained a new member, another daughter, whom they named Meita[51], their seventh child.

Throughout 1913, and the harvest season of 1914, Grandpa was on his own and expanding his truck farming business. It was a labor-intensive occupation but only at certain times of the year and depending upon

---

51 Meita is considered a name of Latvian descent, meaning "daughter." It also has Proto-Indo-European roots, the feminine form of the adjective "meit" meaning "tender, dear, loved."

what type of crop was being grown. Truck farmers in this part of Central Wisconsin grew crops that were not only consumed locally, but sold in cities with large populations. Milwaukee and Chicago were big markets for rural Wisconsin, as they lacked gardens to grow their own produce such as potatoes, onions or cabbage (considered a staple item in the daily meals for so many northern Europeans that had immigrated here.)

These annual crops didn't take years to develop such as fruit trees did before they start to produce. However, preparing the soil was more labor intensive and was done by using horse drawn implements and hand planting. The implement plowed a shallow furrow, then a person sitting on it would drop a seed potato, set an onion or cabbage plant in the soil with appropriate spacing, followed by a part of the same tool that pushed dirt back in the furrow to cover the plant. During the growing season it was necessary to control the weeds but that could be done fairly efficiently with a horse drawn cultivator. Cabbage was probably the easiest of the above mentioned crops to harvest because it grew above ground and didn't have to be dug up before gathering.

Once harvest was completed the truck farmer could find other work to do. Grandpa Charly planted corn or grain during the spring and summer for fall harvest, and gathered hay for the few animals he kept.

In September of 1914 he purchased an additional ten-acre plot of land in the north-west part of Ripon township. This is a curious piece of land as part of the section is divided into twenty or more rectangular parcels, each belonging to different owners.

None of the parcels was more than twenty acres, most were ten or less acres, located in what looks to be marsh land with no road leading to the area. There is no indication that this was a wooded area, which could have suggested the land was purchased for cutting firewood. Local historians told me this area would have been of interest to residents at the time because there was a high probability a new road would pass right near these lands, providing them with public access and driving up the land value over the years. A second and additional good reason was that,

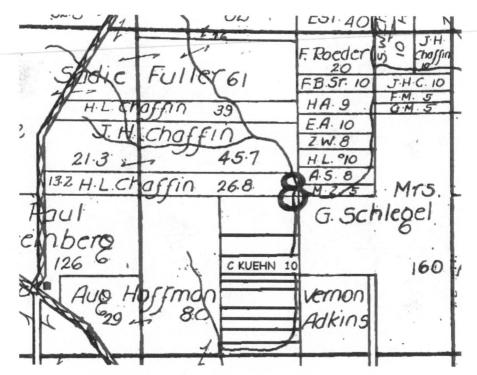

Ripon Township, Section 8, where many small plots of land were located. The wording C.Kuehn 10 indicates my grandfather's 10-acre plot. Notice the small rectangular parcels above and below it. Courtesy Fond Du Lac Public Library

even if that road did not get built, the marsh areas could be drained, leaving a rich loamy soil, ideal for the type of cash crops a truck farmer would grow and for which there was always a market. Plus, the direct railroad connections from Ripon to the large city markets also provided important produce distribution points.

Grandpa Charly's business continued to grow, as did his family. In October of 1915 my grandparents welcomed a daughter, named Grace. Her birth certificate still listed Grandpa's occupation as Truck Farmer while Hulda's occupation continued to be that of housekeeper/wife. By the fall of 1916, my grandparents now had eight children, four boys and four girls, owned a house, a farm and land, and were debt free.

Farmers with horse drawn wagons piled high with cabbage waiting to be loaded into railroad cars. Photo from the Ripon Main Street collection used in "*A Portrait of Ripon*," by David Sakrison and Harry Heileman.

Their frugal living and the hard-working lifestyle learned from their immigrant parents had paid off. These first-generation Americans, although humble and ordinary, were leaving a mark on the identities and the future of their children and grandchildren, and on a small - yet not less relevant scale - on the socio-economic history of the State of Wisconsin.

By 1917, life in the United States was about to change. World War I had been raging in Europe since 1914, a war the United States had managed to avoid being drawn into. But in early 1917, after several U.S. merchant and liner ships traveling to and from Britain (a U.S. ally) had been torpedoed by German forces, killing hundreds of Americans aboard, the U.S. entered the war.

April 2, 1917 - U.S. President Wilson asked Congress for a Declaration of War on Germany.

May 18, 1917 - Congress passed The Selective Service Act giving the President the power of conscription (by a vote of 373 to 50).

June 5, 1917 - Conscription began in the United States (for all men aged 21-30).

One of the many consequences of war, was the toll it would take on the U.S. economy. Beginning in late 1916 and continuing into 1917, inflation figures were expanding monthly, unchecked, at an annual rate approaching 20 percent.[52]

Though they lived in rural Wisconsin, my grandparents and their family were affected by what was going on in this country and the world. There were two main things to worry about. First, the two older boys, Fred (22) and Walter (20), were still single, living at home and subject to the draft[53], making Grandpa Charly face for the first time the same emotional challenges so many other families encountered: how to stand by their country without losing their children; especially when those same children helped sustain the family business which they wholly depended on. Second, and no less important, inflation was impacting Grandpa's truck farming business, with a reduced market for his products due to price increases and, the rising costs for seeds and farm implements, making the future of his work unpredictable.

Fortunately, Fred would not have to go to war. His draft registration shows he was exempt because of a non-specific "rupture" (possibly a hernia.) Walter wasn't required to register for the draft for at least another year, which meant his oldest boys could stay home and continue to help with the family business.

---

52 U.S. Bureau of Labor Statistics, "Table of Historical Inflation Rates by Month and Year, (1914-2015)."

53 Fred's draft registration shows he registered the day the law went into effect listing his occupation as working for his father's truck farming business. Walter, upon reaching his 21st birthday on August 15 of 1918, would have been required to register within the supplemental registration. We know, anecdotally, he received his draft notice but the World War I Armistice was signed before he was required to report to the Army.

In July of 1917, Grandpa used the two lots that made up the Ripon farmstead as collateral for a new loan. It was through much research and conversations with my siblings and cousins, trying to find and fit the pieces of my grandparent's puzzle together, that I've come to believe the money Grandpa Charly borrowed in 1917 was used to start his dray line business, perhaps to purchase a truck and necessary equipment for this type of endeavor rather than using his horse drawn wagon. A truck would be much more common and efficient. Amidst the challenging and uncertain times surrounding them, and what I can only imagine was an incredibly busy life, my grandparents continued to bring children into the world. On September 30, 1918, another daughter, their ninth child, was born. Her name was Verna. A few months later, on the morning of November 11, 1918, Germany signed the long-awaited Armistice ending World War I. *"Hostilities ceased at 11:00am that day, the eleventh day of the eleventh month, November 11, 1918."*[54] Charly's and Hulda's boys would not have to go to war.

In 1921 Grandpa Charly, by then fifty-one and Grandma Hulda, forty-three, were probably satisfied with what they had accomplished in their lives: raising a good family and having a business that prospered. The year however was also marred with sadness when Hulda, pregnant at the time, lost a daughter a few days after giving birth, due to a serious heart defect.[55] Emotionally shaken by this event, and probably thinking of their own mortality, in 1921 they purchased a family plot at Woodlawn

---

54 Armistice Day became a national holiday in 1926 with the name changed to "Veteran's Day" in 1954.

55 The birth certificate, filed after the infant died, indicated she suffered from "Patent foramen ovale" (a hole in the heart that didn't close properly after birth.) There was no surgical procedure to correct the serious physical defect, so the only option was for nature to take its course. The child's name was recorded as "Unnamed Infant" on the birth certificate. Family lore tells the name "Olga" was chosen if the infant had lived. On the gravestone is inscribed only, "INF DAU," 1921.

Back row, Fredrick, Benjamin, Agnes, and Walter. Front row, Clarence, Meita, Charles, Verna, Hulda, Grace and Laura. Kuehn Family Collection.

Cemetery in Ripon with spaces for ten interments, the first being occupied by this infant daughter.

By the end of 1921, the remaining nine children, ranging in age from three years old to twenty-six, still resided at the Griswold Street home. The youngest two children were not yet of school age, but those who were, attended Brown Elementary while in session and helped around the farm, or where needed, as was customary at the time.

During the next few years, the three older boys would leave home to marry and begin to seek their own way in life, working at various occupations. Their oldest daughter Agnes, by then twenty-one years of age, worked as a maid and lived at home, while their youngest son Clarence, my father, had taken over managing Grandpa Charly's business.

As the decade ended, the stock market crashed in late 1929, plunging the United States economy into the years of the Great Depression. By this time, Grandpa Charly was approaching sixty years of age, and I was yet to be born.

CHAPTER 11

Grandpa Charly Kuehn, Part II

Aunt Agnes and Grandpa Charly during a family gathering at the farmstead the year Grandma Hulda died. Kuehn Family Collection.

THE STORY THE CENSUSES TELL

IT NEVER OCCURRED TO ME to ask questions about my family's past while my grandfather, or my aunts and uncles, were still alive. Finding out should have been as simple as asking my father, but we just didn't discuss those things in my family. Not that it was taboo, it just never seemed like interesting conversation material, and my father wasn't the outgoing, share-your-life type person either.

A variety of sources that documented my grandfather's life have allowed me to discover much more about him, sufficient information to help me build a good profile. Over two years I researched census records, city, and county directories, birth certificates, and any vital records that might show his occupation or tell me more about who he really was out there, in the everyday world.

In the United States, censuses are taken every ten years and provide marginally relevant information to the ordinary person. But, censuses also provide a decade by decade picture of people's personal and occupational life. The census data was important to me, specifically the information gathered between 1870 and 1940, so I could build a skeleton story of my grandparents, which I would later corroborate through stories, anecdotes, documents, memories, and keepsakes that remained within my family. One census was missing, and one that I wanted to read dearly: The census of 1890, when Charly would have been 20 years old, before he married Grandma Hulda. I wanted to know how and where he started off in life: What was his first official job? Where did he live? To my surprise though, those records are not available, not in Wisconsin, and not for many U.S. States.

The National Archives stated in one of their publications[56] *"Of the decennial population census schedules, perhaps none might have been more critical to studies of immigration, industrialization, westward migration, and characteristics of the general population than the Eleventh Census of the United States, taken in June 1890. United States residents completed millions of detailed questionnaires, yet only a fragment of the general population schedules and an incomplete set of special schedules enumerating Union veterans and widows are available today. Reference sources routinely dismiss the 1890 census records as "destroyed by*

---

56 National Archives, Prologue Magazine, Spring 1996 Issue, Volume 21, No. 1 "First in the Path of the Firemen, Part 1" by Kellee Blake.

fire" in 1921. Examination of the records of the Bureau of Census and other federal agencies, however, reveals a far more complex tale. This is a genuine tragedy of records--played out before Congress fully established a National Archives--and eternally anguishing to researchers...The 1890 census schedules differed from previous ones in several ways. For the first time, enumerators prepared a separate schedule for each family. The schedule contained expanded inquiries relating to race (white, black, mulatto, quadroon, octoroon, Chinese, Japanese, or Indian), home ownership, ability to speak English, immigration, and naturalization. Enumerators asked married women for the number of children born and the number living at the time of the census to determine fecundity. The 1890 schedules also included a question relating to Civil War service... In March 1896, before final publication of all general statistics volumes, the original 1890 special schedules for mortality, crime, pauperism and benevolence, special classes (e.g., deaf, dumb, blind, insane), and portions of the transportation and insurance schedules were badly damaged by fire and destroyed by Department of the Interior order. No damage to the general population schedules was reported at that time... Despite repeated ongoing requests by the secretary of commerce and others for an archives building where all census schedules could be safely stored, by January 10, 1921, the schedules could be found piled in an orderly manner on closely placed pine shelves in an unlocked file room in the basement of the Commerce Building. At about five o'clock on that afternoon, building fireman James Foster noticed smoke coming through openings around pipes that ran from the boiler room into the file room. Foster saw no fire but immediately reported the smoke to the desk watchman, who called the fire department. Minutes later, on the fifth floor, a watchman noticed smoke in the men's bathroom, took the elevator to the basement, was forced back by the dense smoke, and went to the watchman's desk. By then, the fire department had arrived, the house alarm was pulled (reportedly at 5:30), and a dozen employees still working on upper floors evacuated... After some setbacks from the intense smoke, firemen gained access to the basement. While a crowd of ten thousand watched, they poured twenty streams of water into the building and flooded the cellar through holes cut into the concrete floor. The fire did not go above the basement, seemingly thanks to a fireproofed floor. By 9:45 p.m. the fire was extinguished, but firemen poured water into the burned area past 10:30 p.m. Disaster planning and recovery were almost unknown in 1921. With the blaze extinguished, despite the obvious damage and need for immediate salvage efforts, the chief clerk opened windows to let out the smoke, and except for watchmen on patrol, everyone went home... The morning after was an archivist's nightmare, with ankle-deep water covering records in many areas. Although the basement vault was considered fireproof and watertight, water seeped through a broken wired-glass panel in the door and under the floor, damaging some earlier and later census schedules on the lower tiers. The 1890 census, however, was stacked outside the vault and was, according to one source, "first in the path of the firemen." That morning, Census Director Sam Rogers reported the extensive damage to the 1890 schedules, estimating 25 percent destroyed, with 50 percent of the remainder damaged by water, smoke, and fire... The preliminary assessment of Census Bureau Clerk T. J. Fitzgerald was far more sobering. Fitzgerald told reporters that the priceless 1890 records were "certain to be absolutely ruined. There is no method of restoring the legibility of a water-soaked volume." Four days later, Sam Rogers complained they had not and would not be permitted any further work on the schedules until the insurance companies completed their examination. Rogers issued a state-by-state report of the number of volumes damaged by water in the basement vault, including volumes from the 1830, 1840, 1880, 1900, and 1910 censuses. The total number of damaged vault volumes numbered 8,919, of which 7,957 were from the 1910 census. Rogers estimated that 10 percent of these vault schedules would have to be "opened and dried, and some of them recopied." Thankfully, the census schedules of 1790-1820 and 1850-1870 were on the fifth floor of the Commerce Building and reportedly not damaged. The new 1920 census was housed in a temporary building at Sixth and B Streets, SW, except for some of the non-population schedules being used on the fourth floor. Speculation and rumors about the cause of the blaze ran rampant... Despite every investigative effort, Chief Census Clerk E. M. Libbey reported, no conclusion as to the cause was reached... In 1942 the National Archives accessioned a damaged bundle of surviving Illinois schedules as part of a shipment of records found during a Census Bureau move... In 1953, however, the Archives accessioned an additional set of fragments. These sets of extant fragments are from Alabama, Georgia, Illinois, Minnesota, New Jersey, New York, North Carolina, Ohio, South Dakota, Texas, and the District of Columbia and have been microfilmed... There are no fewer than 6,160 names indexed on the surviving 1890 population schedules. These are someone's ancestors."

Those missing records left a gap of information covering two decades, 1880 until 1900. The 1890 census would have provided valuable pieces for me in Grandpa Charly's life puzzle. Did he live with his parents or with another family as a hired hand? What personal property did he have? Did he own any livestock? Horses? Wagons? What was considered his net worth back then? It's during that twenty-year period that my grandparents had grown up, married, moved to Brandon, worked with his father in Metomen and brought their first three children into the world.

Flashforward, when the 1910 census came along, it recorded that Charly, Hulda, and five children, were living in a "mortgaged" house in Ripon's Ward 2, "the farmstead." By 1920 my grandparents had participated in five censuses. The 1920 census didn't tabulate information on type of residence, whether rented or owned, but we know from memory they were living on the farmstead. Their nine children are listed as living there as well, and Grandpa is still "Self Employed," in the drayage business.

THE FINAL YEARS

Before Grandma Hulda passed away in 1948, Grandpa Charly had already left the daily operations of his drayage business to my father Clarence, his youngest son. None of the other children continued that line of work.

After Grandma Hulda passed, life went on for Grandpa Charly. He continued to regularly attend Sunday services at Immanuel Church[57], and was an active member of the church's German speaking Sunday School class.

---

57 Their church was originally Immanuel Evangelical until 1946 when the Evangelical church merged with the United Brethren denomination after which it was known as Immanuel Evangelical United Brethren church and members were known as "EUBers".

Photo of the Immanuel Evangelical Church of Ripon Men's German Bible Class, 1943. Grandpa Charly is in the top row, right end. Courtesy, Immanuel Evangelical Church, currently Immanuel United Methodist Church, Ripon.

By 1950, the year he turned eighty, Grandpa was the father of nine children, a grandfather to seventeen, and a great-grandfather to six. With such a large family, he was always invited and willingly participated in all gatherings. There were always baptisms, birthdays, anniversaries, graduations, and occasions to celebrate something in the ever-growing Kuehn family. Occasionally, one of his daughters would bring him along when they picked up Aunt Agnes to help them on the farm, giving Grandpa Charly a chance to get away from home and spend a day in the country with them.

There were no longer imperative chores that needed to be done to keep up with his animals or land, and there was no longer a need to provide for his family. With more time to himself now, he thoroughly enjoyed puttering around on the farm and spending countless hours doing things that only mattered to him, that made him feel productive and kept his mind occupied.

CHAPTER 12

Back to The Texas Chief

Tracing my grandfather's journey, I stopped at a rural
railroad crossing between Brandon and Ripon, near
Reeds Corners. Photo by Ed Kuehn, 2017.

WHILE A QUIET ATMOSPHERE REIGNED inside, and mostly everyone slept,
the train sped along through the night. Occasionally I was awakened
by the increasing frequency and volume of the "ding, ding, ding" from
the warning signal as the train approached a crossing. The bright red

flashing lights came too close to the window, startling me every time. In a matter of seconds, the train moved on from the crossing, the frequency of the bells would slow down and the volume would fade away, a perfect Doppler effect. Before falling back to sleep my thoughts would return to why I was headed home, traveling alone on this mighty train.

Although the seats were stiff, and finding a long term comfortable position nearly impossible, at some time during the night I fell into a deep, sound sleep, the exhaustion getting the better of me. In what seemed like just a few minutes later, all the lights in the rail coach turned on, abruptly, waking me. It took me a moment to realize where I was. I checked my duffel bag to make sure it was still in its place. It was. The railroad clacking brought me back into reality and into this journey home. Looking out the window I could see the sun rising and the scenery subtly changing. It was flat land now, planted with corn, as far as my eyes could see. We must have been traveling through northern Illinois. This Texas Chief would arrive at the old Dearborn station in Chicago at 9:15am.

I still had a couple of hours to doze off before we reached the end of the line and the next part of my trip would start. It was early in the morning, but that time of year with longer daylight hours, when the sun rises too early making it impossible to sleep.

It was Wednesday June 6, 1956.

The train slowed down, and at a snail's pace, rolled into the Chicago station. When it came to a halt, and there was nothing to do but get off, I took my bag and made my way to the door. Nobody would be waiting for me here, but I sure would have liked to see a familiar face at a time like this. I hadn't been home in five months, and I missed the comfort of being in my room, the well-known faces, and dynamics of my family, and most of all the good, albeit casual, conversations with my brother Carl and my best friend, Merlin Whitney. I couldn't wait to see them.

Several city blocks separated the Chicago train station from the Greyhound bus station. After sitting on the train for so many hours it felt good to be out, get some fresh air, stretch my legs, and take a walk. The weather was nice, the temperature felt cool after coming from Texas, and the walk had the bonus of not having to pay for a cab fare. I didn't visit Chicago often when we lived in Ripon, Wisconsin, so the hustle and bustle of this big city provided some mental distraction.

The bus station in Chicago was quite lively. People were coming and going at a fast pace, like carpenter ants on a mission. I bought a coach seat ticket to Fond du Lac, Wisconsin, which would give me another three hours of reflection time, setting my arrival for the middle of the afternoon.

As is common with long journeys, the last hours of any trip seem to last forever, the destination never close enough. I was relieved when we finally pulled into Fond du Lac. I couldn't wait for the trip to be over. I needed a bath, some good homemade food, and a decent bed after sleeping upright through the night.

At the first available telephone booth, I placed a collect call to my parent's home in Ripon telling them I had arrived, asking to please send someone to come get me. My brother Carl offered, probably because he missed the companionship we had both enjoyed growing up. I was happy I would see him first - we had so much to catch up on.

Grandpa Charly's funeral was held the following morning, Thursday, June 7, 1956. He passed away quietly at his home on the farmstead after being ill for over a week. His death certificate states the cause of death was coronary occlusion, arteriosclerotic cardiovascular disease, and senility. We arrived at the Evangelical United Brethren church in Ripon an hour or so prior to the service, and met with the rest of the family. I wore my civilian Sunday suit, because there hadn't been time to clean and press my khaki Army uniform after wearing it for the previous twenty-four hours, and, I didn't bring another one as I had departed in a hurry and was traveling with the least amount of baggage possible.

As I entered the church, the brown wooden casket lay solemnly down in front, by the altar - and suddenly I was a boy of twelve again, coming to say goodbye to Grandma Hulda. It was the same church, the same people, and the same emotions building up inside. This would be the last time I would see Grandpa Charly. My memories of his life, which I had been reliving during the long ride home, flashed again through my mind. The knobby hands. The brown felt hat. The suspenders. The buttoned-up flannel shirts. Walking slowly with the aid of his cane. How he patted Old Jim's face before hitching him to the wagon, reminding him of what a good horse he was.

The coffin appeared to gently cradle Grandpa Charly. He lay there with a serene look on his face, his withered gray-brown mustache still there. Grandpa Charly was eighty-five years old when he passed away on Monday, June 4, 1956, After the service, the family and friends followed the hearse in a procession of cars to Woodlawn cemetery, so we could bury him alongside Grandma Hulda and the infant daughter they had lost.

I don't recall the rest of the details of that day, except for bizarrely attending my brother Carl's high school graduation that evening. It was a day of dichotomies, of great sadness and joyous pride. It was a trip packed with many self-doubts and self-realizations. I had recently celebrated my twentieth birthday, leaving my teen years behind. The past three days had been physically and emotionally draining. In a day or so I would be making that long trip back to Texas, giving me more time than I probably wanted to reflect on what had taken place. Thinking about how life goes on, whether the people we love are in it or not. After spending the weekend at home with family and friends, and feeling thankful for the family I had, a part of me felt good heading back to Fort Hood, Texas and to the Army - it gave me a sense of a purpose when life seemed so sad. It would take a while for the sorrow to fade and all these events to find their place in my memories.

Over the years I've come to accept there is so much I will never know about Grandpa Charly. What was his childhood like? How did he fall in love with Grandma Hulda? When did he know it was the time to leave his father's farm and try a business of his own? Did he have self-doubts? How did he manage nine children? What was he passionate about? Did he know he was leaving an everlasting memory in his grandchildren?

I've done the best I could to discover and reconstruct my grandfather Charly's life, to better understand who he really was, and to document his legacy. I am forever grateful for all the things he did for us, and am especially appreciative of the wonderful times we spent with him on his Ripon farm.

Verna and Grace standing on the new car. Grace, on the
right in the photo, wears a short pants romper.[58]

In 1946, WHILE MY GRANDPARENTS were still alive, they assigned the homestead title to their four youngest daughters Laura, Meita, Grace and
Verna. The deed read that the girls were to receive the property for
"mutual love and affection."

---

58 Short pants were taboo and were only considered acceptable in the 1930's when
Hollywood actresses, like Katherine Hepburn began wearing them. http://www.npr.org/
sections/npr-history-dept/2015/04/07/397804245/when-wearing-shorts-was-taboo

There was no written document but it was understood they would provide for them, pay the property taxes, and help with the upkeep of the homestead.

Aunt Agnes was left off the deed for undeclared reasons, though among the cousins we believe it had probably been agreed that because she was the oldest, and unmarried, she could live in the house as my grandparent's caregiver, since the siblings had left to care for their own families.

My grandparent's first son Frederick (Fred), married Marie Hallman and had three children, Arthur, Robert, and Louella. He started off with Grandpa Charly in the drayage business then worked at the Barlow and Seelig Company in Ripon, which would later become Speed Queen/ Alliance Laundry, manufacturing washing machines, until he retired.

Walter, their second son, started off in the drayage family business as well, then served as a rural mail carrier. He later completed mortuary school, and operated his own business as a funeral director. After marrying Laura Zellmer, they had two daughters, Geraldine, and Marceline, who helped me find important details of Grandpa's life for this book. In his later years Uncle Walter moved to Waupun and operated a furniture upholstering business. He also served one term as mayor and taught upholstering at the technical college until his retirement.

Their third child, Agnes, besides taking care of my aging grandparents, would occasionally work as a domestic aid for a few families in Ripon, or help her sisters, who also lived on farms, with canning, watching the children, and preparing meals for crews of farm workers during harvest time. One interesting story related to me was that Agnes married and left home for a time, or had gone off to Chicago for a man, but it didn't work out and she returned home. We don't know why the marriage failed or what exactly happened, but we cousins never knew a husband for her. A wedding ring was found among her valuables after she passed away, and it was thought to have been hers. She lived with my grandparents up until the time of their deaths, after which she moved in with her married sister Laura, and when Laura passed in 1968, Agnes went to live with her sister Meita for a time and later to a senior living facility in Ripon, where she passed away in 1986.

Grandpa Charly and Grandma Hulda's fourth child, Benjamin, also worked in the drayage business, then as a driver for Badger Farm Produce, until he followed his brother Fred to Barlow and Seelig, the employer from which he would retire. Ben married Catherine Lambert and had two boys, Lester, and Harold.

My father, Clarence their fifth child, was the only one in the family who continued to work in the dray business Grandpa Charly had started until he became the sole owner. The company continued to be successful despite the stock market crash in 1929, two years after my father took it over, and with the Great Depression that followed in subsequent years. In 1932, during the depth of the depression, he turned twenty-four and married my mother, Genevieve Tetzlaff, leaving his parent's farmstead to live in a rented house on South Grove Street in Ripon. Their first child, a daughter Alice, was born in 1933 and a second daughter, Elaine in 1935. That same year he bought two lots on Ransom street, building a house (which still stands) on one and using the second lot as a garden. I, Edward, arrived as their third child the following year, in 1936. My brother Carl was the fourth child, arriving in 1938, and completing our family. Sadly, Carl passed away on November 15, 2016, before I had time to finish this book.

My father, ran the dray line business for over twenty years, then he turned to farming as an occupation. He sold the dray business to his nephew Arthur Kuehn who ran the company for another thirty years.

My grandparents sixth child, Laura, worked for a time at a Ripon factory that hired women, and after that as a clerk at Hader's Drug Store. Laura married later in life, to Carl Wille, a gentleman who had lost his first wife and was raising a son as a single parent. She and her husband lived the rest of their lives in Ripon.

Meita, Charly and Hulda's seventh child, stated in the high school yearbook she wanted to become a stenographer after graduating from Ripon High School in 1931, but was instead also employed at one of the many Ripon factories. Meita married Ardin Page making their living on a farm in Green Lake County. They had 2 daughters, Jean who provided me with invaluable photographs and anecdotes throughout my research for this book, and Marilyn.

Grace, my grandparent's eighth child, stated in the Ripon High School yearbook that she wanted to attend "normal" school after graduation. She also worked for a time at a factory in Ripon and later married Lyle Rispalje and lived on a farm in Brandon. Their family consisted of three children, Robert, Philip, and Rebecca; the latter two helped me with input for this book.

My grandparent's ninth child Verna, married Orville Tavs and they had one daughter, Shirley. She was the granddaughter who enjoyed milk toast with Grandpa Charly when staying overnight at our grandparent's home. After they married they owned and operated several different farms in the Ripon, Brandon, and Rosendale area over the years.

I learned through my all my research of Charly and Hulda's life that their family was able to weather the effects of WWI, the Great Depression and WWII because of their thrifty lifestyle, everyone's hard work, cancelling their debts as early as possible, and because Charly had diversified his businesses. Besides truck farming and drayage work, he participated with his son Walter, in the 1930s, in a small company that manufactured burial vaults on his property. I recall seeing the building where the vaults were manufactured when I visited the farm. As an adult, I realized that the family dray business would also have benefited by hauling the vaults to the cemetery where they were to be placed.

Although they all lived frugally for the most part of their lives while on the farm, I discovered that they allowed themselves a token of prosperity. A photo from those years shows a new car parked in the driveway of the farmstead: A 1932 Studebaker Rockne, with the two young girls posed on it. Charly would have been sixty-two years old at the time. Family lore states the car was purchased upon the insistence and financial help of Aunt Laura and Aunt Meita, both who worked full time and still lived at home, to provide the family with a bit of luxury and modern transportation.

In all his life, Charly never worked for a company that provided a pension benefit. Social Security for elderly persons as we know of it today wasn't enacted until 1935 and, despite turning 65 that year he was not eligible.[59] My grandparents had planned for their retirement years by putting money away for when they could no longer earn it.

As the 1930's wore on and before the calendar turned over into the 1940's the United States was again being drawn into the global situation that became World War II. Grandpa Charly, despite that he would turn 70 later that year, was listed in the 1940 census as being an "excavator" in the "construction" trades (probably related to Walter's burial-vault business) along with being a "farmer" again.

After Grandpa Charly died, the house was unoccupied for about a year. The farm land continued to be worked on by my father Clarence, who had taken over Grandpa's farming after Charly lost his horse. In the summer of 1957 the farm was purchased from the four daughters by one of their granddaughters, my sister Alice, and her husband Allen Uecker. Shortly thereafter Alice, Allen, and their toddler Robert, moved onto the farm.

---

59 Quoted from an article "Celebrating Social Security," by Robert Dallek. "Eligibility to receive payments in the initial program was limited, it made no provision for farm workers or domestics or workers in small businesses with fewer than 10 employees. And those who were already past age 65 were also left out of the mix." AARP bulletin, July/August 2015, Vol.56 No. 6, pg. 17.

That summer of 1957 Alice went about making the house into a home while Allen busied himself with cleaning up the farm, removing the farm buildings that were no longer used, and more importantly bringing modern conveniences into the house with an indoor bathroom and running water in the kitchen.

I drive by the property when I find myself in Ripon, out of curiosity and out of nostalgia, each time replaying a different memory of Grandpa Charly and Grandma Hulda, reliving in my mind what has been lost with the passage of time.

ACKNOWLEDGEMENTS

THIS BOOK IS A RESULT of the unconditional support of the following people: Jason Mansmith (Ripon Chamber of Commerce), your enthusiasm, positive energy and determination is contagious, thank you for being there for us. Larry Behlen (Dartford Historical Society), your knowledge, expertise and insights were invaluable. For every question we had, you had a detailed answer. Marjorie Mlodzik (Princeton Historical Society), there has never been a sweeter person to work with, always willing to open up the museum and sit with us (for the sheer pleasure of it) combing through files, allowing us to discover more. Tracy O'Brien and Carol Sachen (Ripon Historical Society) we appreciate your help in finding archived historical documents and allowing us to photograph historical displays. Richard Roeming (Brandon Historical Society), thank you for allowing us to peruse documents and photos to make sure we were accurately describing the era and location. Barb Vande Brink and Marlene Scott (Fairwater Historical Society), thank you for keeping us in the loop with newsletters and giving us access to documents and photos and allowing us to photograph historical displays. Tim Lyke (Ripon Printers), reading through Ripon Commonwealth papers from the early 1900s is an experience we will never forget. Thank you for generously sharing with us that piece of history. Bobbie Erdman (Berlin Area Historical Society), Gayle Schultz (Markesan Historical Society) and Genevieve Best-Dickenson, thank you for reviewing our manuscript, and providing us with detailed and invaluable feedback. Your time and dedication to our project is deeply appreciated. Matt Lirag, thank you for editing our photos, your work brought our manuscript to life. To the Caestecker Public Library in Green Lake, the Fond du Lac Public

Library and the Ripon Public Library, thank you for your personal assistance and unconditional sharing of your reference material, always guiding us to new sources and information that gave us context. So much of what we've learned in your spaces is present in this book. To Ripon Main Street, Inc. for allowing us to use such wonderful turn of the century images, and to the Shops of Water Street in Princeton for being such great supporters of our project.

I would personally like to thank my sisters Alice and Elaine, and to my brother Carl, who was named after Grandpa Charly. To my cousins, especially Jeannie and Marceline, who contributed in different ways to make this book a success. And, to my wife, Sherri, for reading our manuscript, multiple times.
Ed Kuehn

Thank You to the staff and volunteers of the Berlin Area Historical Society, the Brandon Historical Society, the Dartford Historical Society, the Fairwater Historical Society, the Green Lake Conference Center, the Kingston Historical Society, the Markesan Historical Society, the Marquette Historical Society, the Princeton Historical Society, the Ripon Historical Society and the Rosendale Historical Society. You have expanded my mind and education, and your work in preserving the past of rural Wisconsin is priceless. I have enjoyed your company and conversations immensely. Wendy Ruggeri, gracias por tu ayuda y por siempre tenerme fe! And to Cristiano, for your love and support throughout these years.
Linda Ruggeri

BIBLIOGRAPHY

The following books were consulted for this manuscript. Passages used were noted on their corresponding page as footnotes.

1. A *Heritage History of Beautiful Green Lake*, by Robert and Emma Heiple.
2. "A *Portrait of Ripon*," by Ripon Main Street, Inc., pg. 100.
3. A *Settler's* Year, Wisconsin Historical Society Press, 2015, by Kathleen Ernst.
4. American Psychology Association, "Crossroads: The Psychology of Immigration in the New Century" by Carola Suárez-Orozco, PhD, Chair, Dina Birman, PhD, J. Manuel Casas, PhD, Nadine Nakamura, PhD, Pratyusha Tummala-Narra, PhD, Michael Zárate, PhD.
5. *Destination America*, Dorling Kindersley Limited, UK, 2006, Chuck Wills.
6. *Germans, Poles, and Jews: The nationality conflict in the Prussian east, 1772-1914 by* William W. Hagen
7. Pedrick Genealogy Notebooks (Ripon Public Library, Ripon, Wisconsin)
8. *Prussian Netzelanders And other German Immigrants In Green Lake, Marquette & Waushara Counties, Wisconsin by* Brian A. Podoll, C.G.R.S.
9. *Ripon, Images of America* by Amanda Gesiorski, Naomi Jahn and Christian Krueger
10. *Rusty Memories and Ruby Red Wealth*, Roberta A. Erdman
11. *The History of Wisconsin, Volume IV, The Progressive Era, 1893-1914*, by John D. Buenker
12. 1880 Assessment Roll - Personal Property, Town of Princeton for the year 1880 (Princeton Historical Society)
13. *The Lives of Undistinguished Americans as Told by Themselves* by Hamilton Holt (1906).
14. *New Standard Encyclopedia*, Standard Education Corporation, 2006.

15. *The History of Fond du Lac County As Told By Its Place-Names* by Rita Shaw Worthing.
16. *The Writer's Guide to Everyday Life in the 1800s* by Marc McCutcheon, pg. 53.
17. *The Wisconsin News Cookbook,* 1932 Edition. "Wheat Bread", pg. 15-16.